For All

AN ADVENT STUDY OF THE CHRISTMAS STORY

Published by Sacred Holidays. © 2018 Sacred Holidays

If you know someone who is unable to afford this study and you are unable to purchase it for him or her, please see the Discounts page under the Advent tab on www.sacredholidays.com or contact hello@sacredholidays.com for help. It is our desire to ensure that everyone is able to do this study and will not let cost be a barrier.

ISBN 978-1-7328502-0-0

Cover and interior design: Megan Sjuts | Building 07 (www.building07.com)
Edited by Molly Parker

To order additional copies of this resource:
Visit the online shop at www.sacredholidays.com/shop or contact us for bulk orders (over 50 studies) for special pricing and delivery at hello@sacredholidays.com.

Printed in the United States of America

Sacred Holidays, P.O. Box 131476, Spring, TX, 77381

For All

- ☐ **Candle 1:** Light FOR ALL in Darkness
- ☐ **Candle 2:** Lead by His Light
- ☐ **Candle 3:** Light and Love For All
- ☐ **Candle 4:** See A Great Light
- ☐ **Candle 5:** The Light Has Come

CHOOSE #LESSCHAOSMOREJESUS EACH DAY THIS ADVENT

- ☐ **Day 1:** Adam and Eve *with Kara-Kae James*
- ☐ **Day 2:** Prophecies *with Sharon Miller*
- ☐ **Day 3:** Zechariah *with Mandy Arioto*
- ☐ **Day 4:** Genealogy *with Elizabeth Hyndman*
- ☐ **Day 5:** Mary (Jesus's Mom) *with Jandi Harris*
- ☐ **Day 6:** Joseph *with Christina Crenshaw*
- ☐ **Day 7:** The Holy Spirit *with Amber Burger*
- ☐ **Day 8:** Elizabeth *with Jenn Jett Barrett*
- ☐ **Day 9:** Mary's Song and Treasure *with Rebecca Renfrow*
- ☐ **Day 10:** Bethlehem *with Kat Armstrong*
- ☐ **Day 11:** No Room and The Manger *with Lindsay Benedetto*
- ☐ **Day 12:** Jesus *with Sharifa Stevens*
- ☐ **Day 13:** Shepherds *with Rachel Joy*
- ☐ **Day 14:** Angels *with Heather Brock*
- ☐ **Day 15:** Wise Men *with Kelly King*
- ☐ **Day 16:** King Herod and The Scribes *with Molly Parker*
- ☐ **Day 17:** The First Seven Days *with Melanie Dale*
- ☐ **Day 18:** Simeon *with Osheta Moore*
- ☐ **Day 19:** Anna *with Jen Weaver*
- ☐ **Day 20:** For All *with Tia Plum*

CUT ALONG THE DOTTED LINE + USE AS A BOOKMARK TO KEEP YOU ON TRACK THIS ADVENT

SHARE THIS WITH OTHERS!
@SACREDHOLIDAYS | #SACREDHOLIDAYS

Contents

DO THIS BEFORE ADVENT BEGINS

How to Use This Study   10

Reflect & Commit   16

ADVENT CANDLE LIGHT WITH BECKY KISER

Candle 1: Light FOR ALL in Darkness   23

Candle 2: Lead by His Light   29

Candle 3: Light and Love For All   35

Candle 4: See A Great Light   43

Candle 5: The Light Has Come   49

ADVENT STUDY DAYS

Day 1: Adam and Eve *with Kara-Kae James*   57

Day 2: Prophecies *with Sharon Miller*   61

Day 3: Zechariah *with Mandy Arioto*   65

Day 4: Genealogy *with Elizabeth Hyndman*   69

Day 5: Mary (Jesus's Mom) *with Jandi Harris*   75

Day 6: Joseph *with Christina Crenshaw*   79

Day 7: The Holy Spirit *with Amber Burger*   85

Day 8: Elizabeth *with Jenn Jett Barrett*   91

Day 9: Mary's Song and Treasure *with Rebecca Renfrow*   95

Day 10: Bethlehem *with Kat Armstrong*   99

Day 11: No Room and The Manger *with Lindsay Benedetto*   103

Day 12: Jesus *with Sharifa Stevens*   **109**

Day 13: Shepherds *with Rachel Joy*   **113**

Day 14: Angels *with Heather Brock*   **117**

Day 15: Wise Men *with Kelly King*   **121**

Day 16: King Herod and The Scribes *with Molly Parker*   **125**

Day 17: The First Seven Days *with Melanie Dale*   **129**

Day 18: Simeon *with Osheta Moore*   **133**

Day 19: Anna *with Jen Weaver*   **137**

Day 20: For All *with Tia Plum*   **141**

APPENDIX

For Groups and Group Leaders   **148**

About Sacred Holidays   **149**

Contributors + Bios   **150**

10% for Vulnerable Women and Children in Kenya (learn more!)   **158**

Excerpt from *Sacred Holidays: Less Chaos, More Jesus* by Becky Kiser   **161**

Let's Really Stay Friends   **188**

Read the first chapter of *Sacred Holidays: Less Chaos, More Jesus* by Becky Kiser!

Hello

Christmas season is finally here, and if I could use emoticons in this study, I'd have like four rows of heart-eye smiley faces with a few lit up Christmas trees sprinkled in between.

This is my hope and prayer for you this year—that you would celebrate Him more than you ever have before, that you would know He came **FOR ALL.**

I promise to be honest with you throughout this study and not offer you fluffy words that hold little weight. Here's the first thing I'm gonna shoot to you straight—this will be hard. Actually, this will be really hard. Choosing to start a study during this time of year is a little crazy. The good news is, it's not impossible. The other good news is, you are with the right people—we love crazy at Sacred Holidays! We will come together and help cheerlead one another along through this study. We will not quit. We will not have another unfinished study on our shelves that shames us. No, this one we will finish and we will let the Lord mold us into His image as we study His Word and connect with Him and His story.

Ready? Let's get started! This story is **For All,** but it is also for you.

Much love! Mean it.

Becky Kiser

Founder + CEO of Sacred Holidays

P.S. Don't skip the intro sections. You will need 30 minutes to an hour to finish it, so mark off that time. You will be so glad you did. Promise.

P.S. To get the very most out of this study, be sure you are following us on all the things. Plus, we post resources daily that will encourage and equip you, as well as connect you with others.

Follow us on Instagram: @sacredholidays
Like us on Facebook: facebook.com/sacredholidays
Join our private Facebook Group, the Tribe: facebook.com/groups/SacredHolidaysTribe

**And to make it easier for others and for us to find you,
use #sacredholidays and tag @sacredholidays when you post about this study and what God
is teaching you through it!**

DO THIS BEFORE ADVENT BEGINS

HOW TO USE THIS STUDY

Hooray—the study is starting! I know it's pretty typical to skip intro sections, but take the time as you'll likely find this study a little different from what you've done before. Give yourself about 30 minutes to work through the entire intro of this study. However, at the end of that time, we can guarantee you will be ready for Advent!

For many of you, studying God's Word comes second nature, and for others, it can be overwhelming. Knowing how to study God's Word and walk with Him are lacking in our current culture. We tend to take what others have learned, letting social media, podcasts, church, and books become our crutch. These things aren't bad, but they can't be the only places we take in God's Word. So let's study His Word—and that He came **FOR ALL**—this Advent!

Now, let's chat about the study!

PICK YOUR PACE

We want you to choose your flow over the course of Advent. Traditionally Advent begins the four Sundays before Christmas and ends on Christmas day. You are welcome to follow that traditional schedule, or pick your own pace. We've given you 25 days of content: five light study days for when you light your advent candles (typically on those Sundays) and 20 study days. You can start this on December 1st and go 25 straight days. Or you can start in November or halfway through December. There isn't a set way you have to do this study.

Trust the Spirit in you to lead you at your own pace, knowing that shame is not from your Father. I hate to put dates on study days because automatically our check-the-list selves take over. Enter with that come shame and failure, when we don't meet our standards. Fight this. Connecting with Jesus is not a check-the-box thing; it's only a connecting with Jesus thing. Man created Bible studies and calendars and checkbox lists, so give yourself some grace. Deal?

ADVENT CANDLE LIGHTING & LIGHT FOCUSED SCRIPTURE STUDY

If you aren't familiar with Advent, then the process of Advent candles will be a little strange for you, but something I highly encourage! It's a simple practice and will remind you throughout the day of what you are preparing your heart for. I recommend placing your candles where you will see them often. Have some at home, but also consider having some at work. I have small, battery-operated candles that are safe (and cheap!) and great for work spaces or for those with littles at home.

Using Advent candles is simple: just grab five candles and follow the prompts in the study. They can be any color, size, or style. I recommend using battery-operated candles if you have young children in the house or want to have candles at your place of work or dorm room. Traditionally you light the first candle the fourth Sunday before Christmas and then one more each Sunday and the final one on Christmas day. However, follow your own plan if you'd rather. We put these days at the beginning of the study so you can plug it in when you want. If you aren't familiar with this process, I recommend setting out a note on Sundays to remind yourself about it and make it a priority. Then simply follow the prompts and let your heart engage with Scripture on those days.

// **WHERE COULD YOU PUT YOUR ADVENT CANDLES SO YOU SEE THEM OFTEN?**

Keep it simple. You will need five candles, and they can be any size and any color.

// **WHAT SUPPLIES DO YOU NEED? WHEN CAN YOU GET THEM? MARK YOUR CALENDAR.**

For more information about Advent candles, watch the following videos on the Sacred Holidays YouTube channel:
https://www.youtube.com/watch?v=_hLei2SnJGl
https://www.youtube.com/watch?v=-n5FEZrltcc

PRAYER PROMPT TO START EACH SESSION

Every day we start with prayer because learning to talk to our Father is a hard discipline. Fight the temptation to skip this prompt. I use the acronym PRAY and then pause to Wait and Listen.

PRAISE: Thank God for who He is and what He has done—in His Word and all around you.

REPENT: Confess sin—the things that separate us from Him.

ASK: Request things for others, for things going on in the world, or whatever else He brings to mind.

YIELD: Surrender yourself and anything going on in your life today to your Father.

WAIT AND LISTEN: Pause afterwards and listen to see if God speaks back to you. You won't likely hear an audible voice (I never have), but you will experience a knowing. The more you listen the more you will hear that voice in your heart, as the Holy Spirit speaks. And oftentimes we get our response the next time we open His Word!

You might prefer to grab a journal to write out prayers if you need more space. Or you can pray without writing. I do a little bit of both—I jot down key words and then talk to the Father.

DOER OF THE WORD APPLICATION

We can often rush off at the end of time spent in Bible study. When we do this, we keep the knowledge of what we've learned in our heads and even our hearts, but don't let it go to our hands, mouths, or feet. Let's change that this year! After we have studied His Word, let's live out the command found in James 1:22, *"Do not merely listen to the Word, and so deceive yourselves. Do what it says . . ."*

At the end of each day you will see this prompt:

DOER OF THE WORD

How can you apply what you have learned from the Lord today?

This prompt is really centered on taking action on a truth you read about that day and applying it to your own life. The Lord might challenge you to respond somehow, like waking up earlier to get in His Word or pray with more faith. He might correct you, asking you to stop doing something, like gossiping or judging a certain person or group.

There might be some days you have several things you need to do, and other days this stays blank—both are totally fine! The important thing is that you pause and ask the Lord if there is anything you should do.

SOCIAL CHALLENGE

While the Doer of the Word application gets us thinking about areas we need to change in our lives, the Social challenge focuses more on sharing with others what God is teaching you. Don't worry, we aren't going to have you go knock on strangers' doors every day, or even any day for that matter. The intent is way more natural. After you've talked to your Father in prayer, studied His Word, become a doer of His Word, you are ready to tell others! Jesus's final command was to go and make disciples (Matthew 28). Because we love others, we should want to share what is true with them!

The problem is, this often makes us very uncomfortable. We don't want to offend, so we say nothing at all. We fear that sharing something others might not agree with is unloving, so we choose silence instead. Hear me, this is not the best way we can love them. If we really believe what God is teaching us is true, than we should share it with others.

Some days you will have something to tell, other days you won't. The point is that you slow down and ask the Father to give you a courageous heart and brave feet. You can do this!

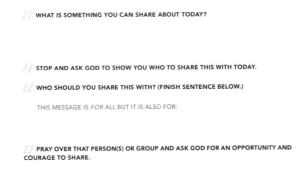

WHAT IS SOMETHING YOU CAN SHARE ABOUT TODAY?

STOP AND ASK GOD TO SHOW YOU WHO TO SHARE THIS WITH TODAY.

WHO SHOULD YOU SHARE THIS WITH? (FINISH SENTENCE BELOW.)

THIS MESSAGE IS FOR ALL BUT IT IS ALSO FOR:

PRAY OVER THAT PERSON(S) OR GROUP AND ASK GOD FOR AN OPPORTUNITY AND COURAGE TO SHARE.

IF YOU SHARE ON SOCIAL MEDIA
BE SURE TO USE #SACREDHOLIDAYS + TAG @SACREDHOLIDAYS.

Some people or groups to consider when deciding who to tell each day:

- People you live with (i.e., family or roommates)
- Co-workers
- Extended family members
- Friends
- Neighbors
- Strangers (look up when you are out and about)
- Social Media friends and followers

We have so many ways we can tell people: in person, text, phone call, email, or whatever way you communicate. You can also share more broadly by posting on social media. During seasons like Christmas, many are more open to hearing these kinds of truths. We know this is true because churches are packed on Christmas. They want to be a part of this story, many just don't know how to find their way to it. You can help by telling them what is true about the Father.

"Go therefore and make disciples of all nations, baptizing them in the name of the Father and of the Son and of the Holy Spirit, teaching them to observe all that I have commanded you. And behold, I am with you always, to the end of the age."
Matthew 28:19-20

STAY CONNECTED

Research shows that when you do something with others, you are more likely to follow through and have better results. It's the reason why Weight Watchers, CrossFit, and all our friends online want us to join their fitness groups for just 30 days—when you do things with others, you are more likely to succeed.

You don't have to do this study alone! I love doing studies with other people for two main reasons: it forces me to stick with it, and I love learning what they have learned. Inevitably, when we start talking, someone will share something I didn't even see. Or their faith encourages me to push into Jesus more, instead of going after Him half-heartedly.

Here are a few ways you can stay connected with others:

1 | Join the Sacred Holidays Tribe (our private Facebook group). This is a great space to go when you want to connect with others who want the same thing out of Advent as you do. There, you can share what God has taught you that day, share prayer requests (we love messy and vulnerable), and be accepted just as you are.

☐ **Go to facebook.com/groups/SacredHolidaysTribe to join and then check the box next to this prompt after you've done that.**

2| **Ask a few friends to join you!** It's never too late because with Amazon Prime, this study can be in your friends' hands in just two days (and for free shipping, too!). Plus, doing this with others is not just so much more fun, but it is so much more beneficial—for them and you! We know life is crazy-busy right now, but you have space and time for this and will not regret the value it brings.

WHO ARE 2-5 FRIENDS YOU COULD TEXT RIGHT NOW AND ASK TO JOIN YOU?

3| **Host or co-host a group—we give you all you need to lead!** If you are interested in hosting a group—online or in person, small or big—check-out our Group page on the Sacred Holidays website. Also, we have a private Facebook Group just for our Group leaders to share tips, prayer requests, and encouragement.

If you don't want to host a group, but you'd love to be in a group, check out our Group page at sacredholidays.com/join-a-group to see if there is one in an area near you.

REFLECT AND COMMIT

Now, let's be realistic. To really do this and do it well, we want to go in strong and prepared. Take the time to complete the reflection and commitment section below.

REFLECT

// **WHAT HAVE BEEN SOME OF YOUR BIGGEST REGRETS FROM PAST ADVENT/ CHRISTMAS SEASONS?**

// **WHY DID YOU DECIDE TO DO THIS ADVENT STUDY?**

// **HOW WOULD YOU DESCRIBE YOUR RELATIONSHIP WITH THE LORD RIGHT NOW? BE HONEST.**

// HOW OFTEN DO YOU SPEND FOCUSED TIME WITH HIM—NOT RUSHED OR ON-THE-GO TIME, BUT STILL AND FOCUSED TIME WITH HIM (SOME CALL THIS A "QUIET TIME")? WHAT DO YOU DO DURING THIS TIME?

// WHAT DOES STUDYING THE WORD OF GOD LOOK LIKE FOR YOU IN THIS SEASON?

// WHAT DOES PRAYER LOOK LIKE FOR YOU IN THIS SEASON?

// WHAT DO YOU HOPE TO GET OUT OF THIS STUDY AND SEASON?

COMMIT

Do you know that most women struggle to spend time with God? They do. Studying God's Word takes effort; it doesn't come easily or naturally. So if you feel frustrated that you are always behind on studies (and you know we don't believe in behind) or feel shame that you never stick with studies, let us help you!

Start with grace. Because He offers it to you freely, give yourself grace and pick up where you left off. If you feel overwhelmed by the study or the season, give yourself grace . . . again (and reach out to us, so we can help you).

//// **WRITE BELOW: "I WILL GIVE MYSELF GRACE."**

With that said, be disciplined. Giving yourself grace is not the same thing as being lazy. You can do this. This may feel hard at times and it will certainly be a challenge, but you've done harder.

//// **WRITE DOWN THREE THINGS YOU'VE DONE THAT ARE HARDER THAN FINISHING A BIBLE STUDY:**

1.

2.

3.

//// **WRITE BELOW: "I WILL NOT QUIT."**

One thing I've realized about myself is how many little obstacles I let take up my time throughout the day. When I choose to be more disciplined in those areas, it creates more time than I realize.

//// **WHEN WILL YOU CHOOSE TO HAVE TIME WITH THE LORD EACH DAY? PICK A TIME AND A PLACE.**

// SET AN ALARM ON YOUR PHONE EACH DAY, SETTING IT 10 MINUTES BEFORE YOU'RE READY TO MEET WITH GOD. TURN ON THE SNOOZE FEATURE SO YOU CAN HIT SNOOZE UNTIL YOU ACTUALLY GET STARTED. INITIAL BELOW WHEN YOU'VE SET YOUR ALARM.

What obstacles might prevent you from making this time a reality? *I want you to think about what distracts you once you're about to sit down or have already sat down. List each one below. Then write down what you can do to eliminate or lessen each distraction. (For example, I know that if I even pick up my phone in the morning I will get lost in the rabbit hole that is Instagram for 20 minutes. So I don't allow myself to touch it until I've spent time with the Lord.)*

OBSTACLES	WHAT CAN YOU DO ABOUT IT?

// SHARE YOUR CHART WITH SOMEONE, OR WITH SEVERAL PEOPLE, AND WRITE THEIR NAMES BELOW. GIVE THEM FULL PERMISSION TO ASK YOU HOW YOU ARE DOING AND HELP HOLD YOU ACCOUNTABLE TO THE GOALS YOU'VE SET.

// WRITE A PRAYER TO THE LORD COMMITTING THIS STUDY TO HIM. ASK HIM TO HELP YOU. ASK HIM TO MOVE IN YOUR HEART AND LIFE DURING THIS LENT SEASON. (YOU CAN WRITE YOUR PRAYER ON THE INSIDE COVER OF YOUR STUDY.)

JUST FOR FUN

(and totally optional, but feel very peer-pressured by us to do this)

We would LOVE to see your group! Will you snap a pic of your group gathering and post it on social media?

Tag **@sacredholidays** and use **#sacredholidays**, so we can see you! Can't wait to see your sweet faces in all the many places you are Gathering!

LIGHT FOR ALL IN DARKNESS

By Becky Kiser

TALK TO GOD

PRAISE God for who He is, what He has done in His Word, and what He is doing in your life now.

_____

_____

REPENT by confessing sin, asking forgiveness (from God and others), and turning a new way.

_____

_____

ASK God for others or about needs you have. He tells us to ask, so share!

_____

_____

YIELD to God by surrendering your day, future plans, and heart's desires to Him.

_____

_____

STOP & LISTEN. Spend some time listening to what God is speaking to your heart.

_____

_____

The first day of Advent is finally here—it's finally Christmas time! You've likely pulled out your Christmas decorations already, finally joining the stores that started decorating in October.

I'm so excited for you this season and for all that's to come! If you haven't already, go back to the beginning section of this study and process through all of it. The reflection portions will help you get what you want out of this study and this season. I promise it will be worth the extra minutes.

// **IF YOU WERE TO SUMMARIZE YOUR MAIN HOPE FOR THIS ADVENT SEASON, WHAT WOULD IT BE?**

// **HOW IS THAT DIFFERENT THAN ALL THE YEARS BEFORE?**

It's possible. Whatever it is you hope happens, it's possible. Likely, as God usually works, it will look differently than you imagined. Isaiah 55:8-9 tells us, *"For my thoughts are not your thoughts, neither are your ways my ways, declares the Lord. For as the heavens are higher than the earth, so are my ways higher than your ways and my thoughts than your thoughts."* The funny thing about God, sometimes slightly irritating, is that His ways are often so very different than what we imagined them to be.

// **TAKE A MOMENT TO PRAY OR WRITE OUT A PRAYER TO GOD ASKING HIM TO FIX "YOUR WAYS" AND "YOUR THOUGHTS" ON HIM, SO THIS ADVENT SEASON WOULD BE "HIGHER" THAN ANYTHING YOU COULD HAVE CREATED ON YOUR OWN.**

This study is called **For All** because we are told the Christmas story is for everyone, and it's the message the angel gave the shepherds the night Jesus was born.

// **WRITE OUT LUKE 2:10-11.**

// GO BACK AND CIRCLE "*FOR ALL.*" THEN WRITE "THE CHRISTMAS STORY IS *FOR ALL.*"

As we study the people surrounding the Christmas story, we know the story didn't just involve them, it was for them—just like it is for you today. And in the same way the "good news" gospel message was "**For All** the people," it is for women everywhere—and that means you! We, as women, tend to focus on what is good for everyone else, forgetting what is true and good for ourselves. Christ came down for you, my friend. He came for all, but He also came just for you.

// EARLIER YOU WROTE "THE CHRISTMAS STORY IS *FOR ALL.*" NOW I WANT YOU TO WRITE, "THE CHRISTMAS STORY IS ALSO FOR ME."

Now that we have that straight, how about we get started with some Bible study?

God has always been about light. It's one of the reasons why I love Advent and Lent so much, they remind us that *"God is light and in Him is no darkness at all"* (1 John 1:5). This week's meditation verse, which you will reflect on before each session, is John 1:1-5, and it tells us that God was in the beginning, that God is light, and that His *"light shines in the darkness, and the darkness has not overcome it."*

I'm a total baby when it comes to darkness. I get freaked-out walking to my own door late at night. I've binged on too many shows on Netflix to know what could be hiding in the dark, even if I'm perfectly safe in my suburb home in Texas. Y'all, when I was 10-years-old and left at home for no more than 20 minutes by myself, watching *The Little Mermaid,* I totally called the cops after the shark tried attacking Ariel. During that scene, I was so certain I heard someone breaking into our house, I ran into the bathroom with our brick-sized wireless phone to call 9-1-1. My parents were so happy when they pulled up just minutes later. Needless to say, I stick to Hallmark movies at night now. Hopefully you are either relating to or laughing at me a little; I'll take either.

// HOW DOES DARKNESS MAKE YOU FEEL? EVEN AS A GROWN-UP DO YOU GET SCARED IN THE DARK?

Now let's talk a little less literal and go with the symbolism that God often uses when teaching us. Darkness represents the unknown, what doesn't yet exist, or has yet to be discovered. For many of us, this can be scarier than what is in broad daylight, fully known.

// WHAT IS UNKNOWN TO YOU TODAY OR IN THIS SEASON OF YOUR LIFE?

Oh friend, I have a giant choke in my throat for you as I'm writing this. I know the burdens are heavy for many of you. Some of you have unknowns that have nearly crippled you. Your darkness is real. Even in a season all about sparkly lights and holiday cheer, we can't escape from what is unknown.

What always helps me is, I put my current struggle up against what is true. I say to myself often, "I can't, but God can." Saying "But God" is one of my most favorite things ever. What may be true of your unknown is redeemed when you add the continuation to your story, "But God."

We will be starting at the very beginning of the Christmas story: the story of Jesus, Immanuel, God With Us. We start in the beginning, right where we first find Him. Before He was wrapped in swaddling clothes and laid down in a manger, He was in the darkness. This story can be a hard one for our logical minds to grasp. But we must believe the truth of it and let Him show Himself to be who He is—the light of the world who has come **For All.** So let's pick-up when all was dark and watch as the One who came creates both light and life.

// READ GENESIS 1:1-31 AND WRITE OUT ALL THAT YOU SEE GOD DO IN THE BEGINNING.

From darkness, God accomplished all of that. What might He also be able to create with your darkness, with your unknown?

I hope this season is one of such hope for you. Whether you are using Advent candles or not, there is light all around you. Let your candles and all the lights that surround you serve as a constant reminder of your Creator God. Take notice of the street lights, the front porch light, the red glow of the brake lights in front of you as they light just the path ahead. Observe the blue glow of your phone and the way its tiny flashlight illuminates your path so you can walk without bumping into things. As you pass the twinkly Christmas lights or join the crowds at the mall under the fluorescent bulbs, remember that God brings light to darkness.

DOER OF THE WORD

How can you apply what you have learned from the Lord today?

SOCIAL CHALLENGE

// **WHAT IS SOMETHING YOU CAN SHARE ABOUT TODAY?**

// **STOP AND ASK GOD TO SHOW YOU WHO TO SHARE THIS WITH TODAY.**

// **WHO SHOULD YOU SHARE THIS WITH? (FINISH SENTENCE BELOW.)**

THIS MESSAGE IS *FOR ALL* BUT IT IS ALSO FOR:

// **PRAY OVER THAT PERSON(S) OR GROUP AND ASK GOD FOR AN OPPORTUNITY AND COURAGE TO SHARE.**

IF YOU SHARE ON SOCIAL MEDIA
BE SURE TO USE #SACREDHOLIDAYS + TAG @SACREDHOLIDAYS.

LIGHT YOUR FIRST CANDLE

IF YOU ARE USING ADVENT CANDLES, LIGHT YOUR FIRST CANDLE.

Before you light your candle, notice the darkness and the way it feels. Then light the candle. Notice what just one light does to the darkness. He brings light! As you pass these candles throughout your day, let them remind you of what the gift of His life brings to you this Christmas—from darkness to light!

LEAD BY HIS LIGHT

By Becky Kiser

TALK TO GOD

PRAISE God for who He is, what He has done in His Word, and what He is doing in your life now.

REPENT by confessing sin, asking forgiveness (from God and others), and turning a new way.

ASK God for others or about needs you have. He tells us to ask, so share!

YIELD to God by surrendering your day, future plans, and heart's desires to Him.

STOP & LISTEN. Spend some time listening to what God is speaking to your heart.

I hope this Advent season has you feeling more connected to the Lord than past holidays. There isn't much we can do about the craziness surrounding this time of year, and we mostly don't want to do much about it. All the other things are not, in themselves, bad; but One thing is better. I hope you've had more of the better this year.

I love hopping on social media during this season and seeing the posts you've tagged us (@sacredholidays) in and/or used #sacredholidays. The wonder of all this, of you, has never once been lost on me. Your stories are constantly on my mind and in my prayers. So to see your actual faces online and hear what is going on in your world . . . it's just the very best. The gospel is such a beautifully uniting thing. Last year we spanned across 48 of the 50 states, 5 countries, and more than 600 women in prison joined us! Who knows how that will change this year? The Lord knows. Even now as I write this, months and months before you will ever hold this study, He foreknew whose hands will be holding it this very day. The details of our stories are so very different, but the hero of our stories is the same—the One who came **For All.**

One of my favorite stories to watch play out in the Bible is God's relationship with the Israelites, His chosen people. I often laugh as I read about them because they are ridiculous. And sadly, the majority of the time I relate to them too. They want to follow God, but then they mess it up—rinse and repeat. I get it. What's beautiful is, the One who created all things out of nothing, the One who sent His Son, Immanuel, is also the One who never abandoned the Israelites. In Exodus 13 and 14 we find the Israelites finally free. For hundreds of years they would've answered the "What is your unknown?" with "When will I finally be free?" But God. He knew they would be in a new unknown, not knowing what would happen next.

/// **READ EXODUS 13:21-22 AND WRITE HOW GOD LEAD THEM.**

He leads with His light, in this case a cloud by day and a pillar of fire by night. God knows you don't know the way and He wants more than anything to show you.

Sometimes that light leads to an easy path; that's what the Israelites thought would happen, I'm sure. But in Exodus 13 the Israelites stood there finally free, lead by a cloud by day and pillar of fire by night, but trapped by the Red Sea. Why would God do this? Then our Isaiah 55:8-9 God said to them in Exodus 14:13-14, "Fear not, stand firm, and see the salvation of the Lord, which he will work for you today. The Lord will fight for you, and you have only to be silent." He did fight for them. Moments later, that sea parted in two and every single one of them made it safely to the other side. They were finally free and all that stood in the way between their Promised Land was a desert. Moses didn't lead them across that sea, God lead them.

/// **READ EXODUS 14:24-25 AND WRITE DOWN WHAT ELSE GOD'S LIT UP PRESENCE DID.**

This is both wild and absolutely true—Jesus was conceived by the Holy Spirit. God's presence went before them and He stuck to His word when He said He would fight for them (14:14). We can count on His light because He has always provided it.

// **WHEN WAS THERE A TIME YOU EXPERIENCED GOD LEADING YOU THROUGH YOUR WILDERNESS OR DARKNESS?**

I often wish that God's presence was as obvious as a cloud or a pillar of fire, but that is rarely the case. However, He has given us a different guide who is always with us.

// **READ JOHN 14:16 AND 26-27, AND WRITE DOWN WHAT JESUS GIVES US INSTEAD OF A CLOUD AND PILLAR OF FIRE. THEN RECORD WHAT IT WILL DO.**

A pillar of fire and a cloud are pretty cool, but Jesus gives us a Helper, the Holy Spirit. This isn't something you earn like badges on a girl scout vest. The moment you believe in Jesus and choose to follow Him, the Holy Spirit is with you forever. Sometimes we think of this as one of those images of the devil and an angel sitting on the shoulders of characters in our favorite cartoons. This isn't exactly how it goes. We are told the Spirit, our Helper, teaches us "all things" so that we can remember what Jesus said. Jesus refers to the Holy Spirit as our peace, which is different than the peace the world offers.

Think back to what you answered above regarding a wilderness or darkness in which you find yourself. Even in the midst of that, your Helper is there. I think of the time the Holy Spirit lead Jesus into the wilderness to be tempted (Matthew 4:1-11). The Holy Spirit might lead us to unusual places; it seems to be His character. He lead Jesus to the wilderness to be tempted by satan, and He lead the Israelites to the edge of the Red Sea with their enemies chasing after them. Both seem like impossible situations, much like your own situation. But God. He uses the Spirit to teach us and help us take an impossible situation and work a miracle or ground us further in our faith.

// **HOW HAVE YOU SEEN THE SPIRIT DO THIS IN THE PAST? DOES IT GIVE YOU GREATER CONFIDENCE IN THE PRESENT THAT HE WILL DO IT AGAIN?**

As you light today's candle and see the light begin to get just slightly brighter, let it remind you this week that He has sent you a Helper to lead you by His light.

LIGHT YOUR SECOND CANDLE

IF YOU ARE USING ADVENT CANDLES, LIGHT YOUR SECOND CANDLE.

If you have an extra moment today, play the song "Do It Again" by Elevation Worship. Let those words build your faith that He was there in the wilderness with the Israelites leading them by His light, just as He was in the wilderness with Jesus leading Him. He will lead you too; it's who He is, not just what He does. Call out to your Helper today. Proclaim to Him, as you sing these words, that you trust Him and know that He is always faithful to lead you to His light.

DOER OF THE WORD

How can you apply what you have learned from the Lord today?

SOCIAL CHALLENGE

// WHAT IS SOMETHING YOU CAN SHARE ABOUT TODAY?

// STOP AND ASK GOD TO SHOW YOU WHO TO SHARE THIS WITH TODAY.

// WHO SHOULD YOU SHARE THIS WITH? (FINISH SENTENCE BELOW.)

THIS MESSAGE IS *FOR ALL* BUT IT IS ALSO FOR:

// PRAY OVER THAT PERSON(S) OR GROUP AND ASK GOD FOR AN OPPORTUNITY AND COURAGE TO SHARE.

IF YOU SHARE ON SOCIAL MEDIA
BE SURE TO USE #SACREDHOLIDAYS + TAG @SACREDHOLIDAYS.

LIGHT AND LOVE FOR ALL

By Becky Kiser

TALK TO GOD

PRAISE God for who He is, what He has done in His Word, and what He is doing in your life now.

REPENT by confessing sin, asking forgiveness (from God and others), and turning a new way.

ASK God for others or about needs you have. He tells us to ask, so share!

YIELD to God by surrendering your day, future plans, and heart's desires to Him.

STOP & LISTEN. Spend some time listening to what God is speaking to your heart.

You are officially halfway through with Advent! I'm so very proud of you. We've talked before about how this is a crazy time to start a Bible study, but it is also the perfect time. I'm so very proud of you for prioritizing this and not letting the craziness of the season overtake what matters most this time of year.

What a perfect time to renew your commitment to this season and to this study. Maybe the past two weeks were magical or maybe all those good intentions fell flat. It doesn't really matter; what matters is today. Our God is a God of new beginnings, so let's take some of that grace for ourselves today, picking up right here. If you thought the past two weeks were crazy, just you wait—these final weeks before Christmas can get a little chaotic, can't they?! So, let's take a moment to choose #lesschaosmoreJesus before we get started on today's study.

// **WHAT'S ONE THING YOU'D LIKE TO BE DIFFERENT DURING THE REMAINDER OF ADVENT? (THIS MIGHT INCLUDE YOUR ATTITUDE, PERSPECTIVE, COMMITMENT TO THIS STUDY, SPENDING HABITS, ETC.)**

// **WHAT CAN YOU DO TO INCREASE THE LIKELIHOOD OF THIS HAPPENING?** *(FOR EXAMPLE, IF YOU WROTE DOWN YOU WOULD LIKE TO BE MORE DISCIPLINED TO DO THIS STUDY, THEN MAYBE YOU NEED TO SET YOUR ALARM A LITTLE EARLIER OR SAY NO TO SOCIAL MEDIA UNTIL YOU'VE FINISHED BIBLE STUDY. BE SPECIFIC AND PUSH YOURSELF. CONSIDER SHARING THIS WITH OTHERS TO HELP ENCOURAGE AND CHALLENGE YOU TO DO IT.)*

Alright, we are ready to go! Let's pick up right here, starting on my most favorite day yet—the reason for the title of this study!

// **WHETHER YOU ARE ARTISTIC OR NOT, I WANT US TO CREATE A LITTLE VISUAL OF WHAT'S HAPPENED SO FAR AND WHERE ALL THE CHARACTERS OF OUR STORY FIT IN. IN THE SPACE BELOW, DRAW (STICK FIGURES WELCOME) THE FOLLOWING PLACES AND CHARACTERS: JOSEPH, MARY, MANGER, JESUS, AND SHEPHERDS. (FLIP BACK TO LUKE 2 IF YOU NEED A REFRESHER.)**

I love Christmas programs or movies that share the Christmas story, but oftentimes they downplay reality. It wasn't a glamorous story. There were no fog machines, flashing lights, or well-trained animals parading around. Sometimes we forget this as we attempt to entertain or reach others in a relevant way. Again, none of these things are bad, as long as Hollywood (or church productions) don't replace the reality of Scripture in our lives.

These were just ordinary moments: a couple paying taxes, a newborn baby being swaddled, and shepherds doing their job in a field. Then something happens to let everyone know this was no ordinary moment, not even close!

// **READ LUKE 2:8-14 AND SUMMARIZE WHAT THE ANGEL TOLD THE SHEPHERDS IN VERSES 10-12.**

It's always so endearing to me how often angels first say *"fear not"* when they come to someone. They had to know their appearance alone would freak people out!

// **GO BACK TO YOUR DRAWING AND ADD THE ANGEL AND THE GLORY OF THE LORD SHINING (OBVIOUSLY YOU HAVE CREATIVE FREEDOM HERE, AND REMEMBER, STICK FIGURES ARE WELCOME).**

I want us to focus on three things the angel said:

1. The angel brought "good news."

I hate it when people leave a message or text with something like, *"Call me. I need to talk to you."* Maybe it's the insecurity or people pleaser in me, but I always assume the worst. (Tell me I'm not alone. I so wish I could insert the laughing emoticon face here. Ha!) I hate teasers, and the control freak in me really struggles with surprises, unless I have no clue the surprise is coming. And you already know from the first day how I feel about darkness. So if I was a shepherd working the night shift and an angel came up to me, I'd freak out.

The angel knew how most people would react (probably a little more normal and less dramatic than me), but I'm going to assume we'd all freak out nonetheless. So I love how the angel and our Father decided to start off with *"Fear not, for behold, I bring you good news . . ."*

2. This "good news" is of "great joy."

This wasn't just any good news, it was the kind that would bring about great joy.

// CAN YOU THINK OF THE LAST TIME YOU FELT GREAT JOY? DESCRIBE WHAT HAPPENED AND WHAT GREAT JOY FELT LIKE.

Sometimes as good as good news is, it just feels good. This news brought great joy.

It's easier to understand good news when we think about what Jesus has brought into our lives. But let's remember, at this time there wasn't Jesus. There was prophecy and there was Judaism; there was God and there were His people. But there was not yet a Savior. God was there, but God was not Immanuel, God with us, yet. Not until this very moment did they find out the One they'd waited for and hoped for had finally come. This was the best kind of news, the kind that brought the greatest of joy.

3. The "good news of great joy" is "for all the people."

What makes this message from the angel crazy-awesome is that it proclaimed *"good news"* of *"great joy"* that was *"for all the people."* Not some of the people or even most people, but *"for all the people."*

// READ JOHN 3:16-17 AND WRITE OUT WHO GOD LOVED (VERSE 16).

You see, the Christmas story is bigger than just finding a baby in a manger; it's about a baby who was sent to save us all. God loved the whole world. He didn't just love Jews. He didn't just love men. He didn't just love the righteous. He loves the whole world—every single person. Then He gave the biggest act of grace to us—He said, *"Whosoever believes in Him should not perish but have eternal life."* Whosoever. Anyone who believes will be saved!!!

This is why the angel was so excited about this good news that was sure to bring great joy!

// WRITE "FOR ALL THE PEOPLE" BELOW.

// NOW, WRITE OUT PEOPLE YOU ONLY SEE ON A WEEKLY BASIS. GO THROUGH YOUR DAY AND YOUR WEEK AND WRITE OUT EVERY NAME. IF YOU AREN'T SURE OF THEIR NAMES, WRITE OUT SOMETHING THAT MAKES YOU THINK OF THEM (I.E., THE CHECK-OUT LADY AT TARGET, BARISTA AT STARBUCKS, GREETER AT CHURCH, MAIL PERSON AT WORK, ETC.).

// NEXT, THINK OF PEOPLE WHO YOU MIGHT NOT SEE EVERY DAY, BUT YOU'LL DEFINITELY BE SEEING OVER THE NEXT COUPLE WEEKS AND OVER THE CHRISTMAS HOLIDAY. WRITE THEIR NAMES BELOW.

// NOW GO BACK AND FOR EACH NAME, SAY IT OUT LOUD (OR IN YOUR HEAD IF YOU CAN'T SPEAK OUT LOUD RIGHT NOW), "THE GOOD NEWS OF GREAT JOY IS FOR _____." (FILL THEIR NAME IN THE BLANK.) DO THIS FOR EACH PERSON.

Pretty wild, isn't it? The moment the angel told those shepherds that the best thing that could ever happen was happening, that the Savior had come, is beyond amazing! And He's for everyone, a reality that's easy to forget in our safe Christian bubbles. We forget that everybody is included in the angel's message. We get caught up in the hustle and bustle of the holidays and just plain forget. Or the times we do remember, we get scared because we don't want to offend or look like a fool, so we stay quiet. So we settle for loving people with our actions, never speaking a single word of this message.

// WHEN WAS THE LAST TIME YOU TOLD SOMEONE THE "GOOD NEWS OF GREAT JOY" ABOUT JESUS?

Hear me, there is no shame or guilt in what you've done before. But let's not let this holiday pass without sharing. Let's not let our pastors at the Christmas Eve service be the only ones who are sharing this message. Let's not let that verse we re-share on Facebook be the only good news our friends hear from us. Let's be the messengers this year! Let's be intentional about showing and sharing the *"good news of great joy that will be for all the people . . . a Savior, who is Christ the Lord."*

// LOOK OVER THAT LIST YOU MADE ABOVE AND ASK GOD TO GIVE YOU BOTH OPPORTUNITY AND COURAGE TO SHARE THIS GOOD NEWS WITH THEM.

LIGHT YOUR THIRD CANDLE

IF YOU ARE USING ADVENT CANDLES, LIGHT YOUR THIRD CANDLE.

The light is getting brighter. This light we know is for all in the darkness (candle 1). This light we are lead by is with us today (candle 2). And this light reminds us that He came for all and loves all (candle 3). Be lead by His light this week, dear friend. He came for all but He also came just for you.

DOER OF THE WORD

How can you apply what you have learned from the Lord today?

_____

_____

_____

_____

SOCIAL CHALLENGE

// **WHAT IS SOMETHING YOU CAN SHARE ABOUT TODAY?**

// **STOP AND ASK GOD TO SHOW YOU WHO TO SHARE THIS WITH TODAY.**

// **WHO SHOULD YOU SHARE THIS WITH? (FINISH SENTENCE BELOW.)**

THIS MESSAGE IS _FOR ALL_ BUT IT IS ALSO FOR:

// **PRAY OVER THAT PERSON(S) OR GROUP AND ASK GOD FOR AN OPPORTUNITY AND COURAGE TO SHARE.**

IF YOU SHARE ON SOCIAL MEDIA
BE SURE TO USE #SACREDHOLIDAYS + TAG @SACREDHOLIDAYS.

SEE A GREAT LIGHT

By Becky Kiser

TALK TO GOD

PRAISE God for who He is, what He has done in His Word, and what He is doing in your life now.

REPENT by confessing sin, asking forgiveness (from God and others), and turning a new way.

ASK God for others or about needs you have. He tells us to ask, so share!

YIELD to God by surrendering your day, future plans, and heart's desires to Him.

STOP & LISTEN. Spend some time listening to what God is speaking to your heart.

Knowing these final days before Christmas are extra crazy, I will keep it simple today without watering things down. I'm sure you have much to do and I want you to soak up all the whimsy, joy, and crazy of this week. Our motto is #lesschaosmorejesus, but we don't want no chaos. There is something exciting about the chaos of the holidays too. However, let's be women who focus and choose more Jesus, even though chaos is inevitable. So let's embrace it along with embracing more Jesus! Deal?

Six years ago I stood at a Christmas Eve service, candle held up, singing *"Silent Night,"* when I realized I had missed it, I had missed Jesus. I vowed to not let that happen again, and that year, I actually meant it. Each year since has gotten better; each year I learn more. I see and savor the coming of Jesus more and more. I learn what works and what doesn't. I'm not sharing this to toot my own horn. I hope my story brings hope to yours. I've learned to give myself and others more grace during this season. As women we can be unfathomably harder on ourselves than is ever justified. Baby steps, my friend, baby steps. Because I've never once gotten Advent "right," I run a grace-filled ministry that is all about making holidays more Christ-focused. After all, there is no such thing as getting it right. So grace to you, my friend.

Today we go back to the very beginning, to one of the early prophecies of Jesus.

// **READ ISAIAH 9:2, 6 AND WRITE IT OUT BELOW.**

Today we are just going to talk to our God, telling Him how awesome He is and how much we needed Him to come. How grateful we are that He came to save us. We are going to divide up our prayer into four parts; follow the prompts below.

// **THANK GOD FOR BEING A *"WONDERFUL COUNSELOR."* TELL HIM ALL THE WAYS HE HAS BEEN A *"WONDERFUL COUNSELOR"* FOR YOU. SHARE WITH HIM THE WAYS YOU STILL NEED HIM TO BE ONE TODAY. MEDITATE ON THOSE WORDS, *"WONDERFUL COUNSELOR,"* AND ASK GOD TO SHOW HIMSELF IN THIS WAY MORE AND MORE.**

// THANK GOD FOR BEING A *"MIGHTY GOD."* TELL HIM ALL THE WAYS HE HAS BEEN A *"MIGHTY GOD"* FOR YOU. SHARE WITH HIM THE WAYS YOU STILL NEED HIM TO BE ONE TODAY. MEDITATE ON THOSE WORDS, *"MIGHTY GOD,"* AND ASK GOD TO SHOW HIMSELF IN THIS WAY MORE AND MORE.

// THANK GOD FOR BEING AN *"EVERLASTING FATHER."* TELL HIM ALL THE WAYS HE HAS BEEN AN *"EVERLASTING FATHER"* FOR YOU. SHARE WITH HIM THE WAYS YOU STILL NEED HIM TO BE ONE TODAY. MEDITATE ON THOSE WORDS, *"EVERLASTING FATHER,"* AND ASK GOD TO SHOW HIMSELF IN THIS WAY MORE AND MORE.

// THANK GOD FOR BEING A *"PRINCE OF PEACE."* TELL HIM ALL THE WAYS HE HAS BEEN A *"PRINCE OF PEACE"* FOR YOU. SHARE WITH HIM THE WAYS YOU STILL NEED HIM TO BE ONE TODAY. MEDITATE ON THOSE WORDS, *"PRINCE OF PEACE,"* AND ASK GOD TO SHOW HIMSELF IN THIS WAY MORE AND MORE.

This is the One we celebrate today, tomorrow, and every day—*"For to us a child is born . . . and his name shall be called Wonderful Counselor, Mighty God, Everlasting Father, Prince of Peace."*

LIGHT YOUR FOURTH CANDLE

IF YOU ARE USING ADVENT CANDLES, LIGHT YOUR FOURTH CANDLE.

The light grows brighter as we near the One who is wonderful, mighty, everlasting, and peace. Just like the room that holds our candles, nothing about the table or chairs or pictures on the wall really changes. We're just seeing everything now in a new light. Same with our circumstances and burdens. The light of Jesus gives us new eyes. This is how followers of God can go through the most heart-wrenching of times and through choking sobs of grief and still feel peace. What was once scary, unknown, and lonely is now made peaceful and always known by our Counselor, God, Father, and Prince. Things may not change, but our focus most certainly has.

I commission you today to be Isaiah 9:2: "The people who walked in darkness have seen a great light; those who dwelt in a land of deep darkness, on them has light shined." I hope as you thanked your Father for being all those things, you've seen how His light has shone on your darkness. Praise God! Let's continue celebrating that He has come FOR ALL, but He has also come just for you.

DOER OF THE WORD

How can you apply what you have learned from the Lord today?

_____

_____

_____

_____

SOCIAL CHALLENGE

// **WHAT IS SOMETHING YOU CAN SHARE ABOUT TODAY?**

// **STOP AND ASK GOD TO SHOW YOU WHO TO SHARE THIS WITH TODAY.**

// **WHO SHOULD YOU SHARE THIS WITH? (FINISH SENTENCE BELOW.)**

THIS MESSAGE IS *FOR ALL* BUT IT IS ALSO FOR:

// **PRAY OVER THAT PERSON(S) OR GROUP AND ASK GOD FOR AN OPPORTUNITY AND COURAGE TO SHARE.**

IF YOU SHARE ON SOCIAL MEDIA
BE SURE TO USE #SACREDHOLIDAYS + TAG @SACREDHOLIDAYS.

THE LIGHT HAS COME

By Becky Kiser

TALK TO GOD

PRAISE God for who He is, what He has done in His Word, and what He is doing in your life now.

REPENT by confessing sin, asking forgiveness (from God and others), and turning a new way.

ASK God for others or about needs you have. He tells us to ask, so share!

YIELD to God by surrendering your day, future plans, and heart's desires to Him.

STOP & LISTEN. Spend some time listening to what God is speaking to your heart.

Merry Christmas, my friend!!! As much as I love being with my family on this day, it's always one of my most favorite days to scroll my newsfeeds (especially our #sacredholidays hashtag feed, so please use that so we can see your day today).

We've gone over a lot the past few weeks. We've studied God's Word and learned from others. We've prayed and meditated on Scripture. We've sabbathed and been doers of the Word. I thought it would be helpful for us to recap the story.

// **TAKE THE TIME TO SUMMARIZE THE STORY WE'VE TOLD OVER THE PAST THREE WEEKS. DO THIS YOUR WAY—YOU CAN WRITE OUT THE NARRATIVE, USE BULLET POINTS, DRAW IT OUT, OR WHATEVER WAY WILL HELP IT BECOME A COLLECTIVE STORY. BUT TAKE THE NEXT FIVE OR SO MINUTES TO THINK THROUGH WHAT WE'VE READ. BE SURE TO INCLUDE: CREATION, ADAM AND EVE, ISAIAH, ZECHARIAH, MARY, JOSEPH, DAVID, THE GENEALOGY OF JESUS, THE HOLY SPIRIT, ELIZABETH, MICAH AND CAESAR AUGUSTUS, THE INN AND MANGER, BABY JESUS, THE SHEPHERDS, THE ANGEL AND THE HEAVENLY HOSTS, THE WISE MEN, KING HEROD AND THE SCRIBES, THE BEGINNING OF JESUS'S LIFE, SIMEON, AND ANNA.**

I hope that was fun for you to recall the story you've spent so much time the past Advent season learning. I hope each of those people and parts of the story mean more than they ever have.

This next part will take a little bit of time, but I hope it is really sweet. If you are spending your day with others, consider inviting them to read this story with you. Otherwise, soak in this alone time with just you and your Savior who has come.

// **READ THE CHRISTMAS STORY: LUKE 1:5-2:38 AND MATTHEW 1:1-2:12. IT MIGHT BE HELPFUL TO READ IT IN A TRANSLATION YOU AREN'T FAMILIAR WITH IT. I WOULD RECOMMEND THE MESSAGE BECAUSE IT FLOWS LIKE A STORY REALLY WELL (IT'S ON THE BIBLE APP FREE). IF YOU HAPPEN TO NOTICE ANYTHING FROM THE STORY WE DIDN'T TOUCH ON THE PAST FEW WEEKS, NOTE IT BELOW.**

Remember our first day together? We went back the beginning of the story in Genesis 1 and saw God form everything out of nothing, light from darkness. We read John 1:1-5 testifying that, "The light shines in the darkness, and the darkness has not overcome it." And also 1 John 1:5, "God is light and in Him is no darkness at all." With each week, as we get closer to the coming Savior, the light increases too.

I hope the symbolism of this strikes you at some point today. The Light has come. His plan has always been to come, as Savior, for all. Let's wrap up this study with proclaiming with the angel what it is we celebrate.

// **WRITE OUT LUKE 2:10-12,14. (YES, ALL OF IT.)**

// **NOW WRITE BELOW: "THIS STORY IS FOR ALL. THIS STORY IS FOR ME."**

I always hate to say goodbye. I'm always tempted to drag this on longer so we can stay together just a tad bit longer. It has been such an honor that you'd share your Advent with me and our team.

I love you. Mean it.

XO, Becky

P.S. I hope you stay involved on social media so we can get to know you more. Let's make it a two-way friendship; comment on our stuff so we can get to know you. We want to connect with you, so don't let your thumb scroll by.

LIGHT YOUR FIFTH & FINAL CANDLE

IF YOU ARE USING ADVENT CANDLES, LIGHT YOUR FIFTH CANDLE.

Before you light your candle, notice the darkness and the way that feels. Then light the candle. Notice what just one light does to the darkness. He brings light! As you pass these candles throughout your day, let them remind you of what the gift of His life brings to you this Christmas— from darkness to light!

DOER OF THE WORD

How can you apply what you have learned from the Lord today or this Advent season?

_____

_____

_____

_____

SOCIAL CHALLENGE

// **WHAT IS SOMETHING YOU CAN SHARE ABOUT TODAY?**

// **STOP AND ASK GOD TO SHOW YOU WHO TO SHARE THIS WITH TODAY.**

// **WHO SHOULD YOU SHARE THIS WITH? (FINISH SENTENCE BELOW.)**

THIS MESSAGE IS _FOR ALL_ BUT IT IS ALSO FOR:

// **PRAY OVER THAT PERSON(S) OR GROUP AND ASK GOD FOR AN OPPORTUNITY AND COURAGE TO SHARE.**

IF YOU SHARE ON SOCIAL MEDIA
BE SURE TO USE #SACREDHOLIDAYS + TAG @SACREDHOLIDAYS.

ADVENT STUDY DAYS

ADAM & EVE

By Kara-Kae James

TALK TO GOD

PRAISE // REPENT // ASK // YIELD // STOP & LISTEN

"Sin messed everything up, everything up, OH NO!"—my kids' latest favorite song, sung loudly from the back seat. Not much beats the honesty and simplicity of children's songs.

It's so true—this world wasn't supposed to be filled with evil, pain, and darkness. The story started out quite a bit differently. When you read the first couple of chapters in Genesis, don't you wish time could stand still, letting the story begin and end there? The beauty in the Garden of Eden was a perfect connection with God. We were designed from the beginning of time to have intimacy with God.

// DESCRIBE WHAT LIFE MIGHT HAVE BEEN LIKE FOR ADAM AND EVE IN THE BEGINNING (BEFORE TAKING A BITE OF THE FRUIT FROM THE FORBIDDEN TREE).

Unfortunately, sin created a barrier between us and God, distorting what intimacy with Him was meant to look like. Sin really did mess everything up! When Adam and Eve sinned, the original plan was destroyed. But as my kids continue with their little song, a song I just can't get out of my head—"But that's not where it ends; God will make it okay, make it okay, OH YEAH!!"—I'm reminded that although the beginning of the story can be a little painful and depressing to read about, the story doesn't end there. God has written a much greater story for us and it starts all the way back at the beginning.

// READ GENESIS 3:1-15 AND SUMMARIZE WHAT YOU READ BELOW.

Here we learn a few things about sin. First, sin lies to us. It tells us that it will be worth it in the end. When Eve saw the fruit and heard the lies, she wanted to believe it was truth. She wanted to believe she would not suffer consequences and everything would be just fine. That's the lie sin told her, thus destroying what she had with God.

Second, sin tempts but can't force. The enemy has no control over us as children of God. Satan cannot force us to do anything we don't want to do. He did not force Eve to eat the forbidden fruit and betray God; it was her own choice.

Next, we see that sin leads to shame. Once Adam and Eve made the choice to be disobedient, they tried covering themselves to hide from what they had done. They now realized they were naked and wanted to hide from their shame. After Adam and Eve made coverings for themselves by sewing together fig leaves, God's voice was heard in the Garden— an audible representation of His power. We are shown here a glimpse of what it was supposed to be like before sin broke their intimate relationship with God. Before their sin, they would have ran to Him in joy! Now when they heard His voice, they hid from Him, full of shame and afraid of what would happen.

And finally we see how sin comes with great consequence. They thought surely eating a piece of fruit couldn't cause harm, but God told them beforehand of their consequences. They had no idea their sin would take them down a deep spiral.

// READ GENESIS 4:25-26 AND WRITE OUT THE LAST SENTENCE OF VERSE 25.

God shows us incredible things about who He is in the beginning of our story with Him. When He could have turned away from His children or destroyed them, He gave them a second chance. He took care of them as a loving Father, clothing them, providing for them, and giving them more than they deserved.

From that day in the Garden, Adam and Eve were no strangers to pain and the consequences of their choices. They faced heartbreak as one of their own children killed his brother, and they cried out to the Lord for another child. God once again came through to comfort and bless them with another child they named Seth (Genesis 5:3). From Seth, a lineage would begin to set in motion the course to bring the Messiah, the one who will make everything new. This is where we begin to see the redemption story of Adam and Eve: God's unfolding plan to cover their sin, which led to the coming of a Savior to cover us all.

// DO YOU FEEL LIKE YOU'VE EVER MADE A BAD CHOICE THAT YOU JUST COULDN'T MAKE RIGHT? SHARE HOW GOD HAS BLESSED YOU EVEN THROUGH THOSE BAD CHOICES.

There are times our bad choices make us feel like we are spiraling and nothing can be made new again in our lives. But God always has a bigger plan! His redemptive plan will always be better than we ever imagined. Did Adam and Eve deserve another child after turning their backs on God? Probably not. But not only was Seth a child, but a covering of redemptive grace on the path toward a Savior who would wipe away all sin. Even when our sin seems trivial, it causes brokenness and disconnection from God. And just because the story didn't go the way God had planned in the Garden, He set everything on track to bring us back to Himself. God gave us the greatest gift of all, a way to connect with Him once again and set the story back to the way it was always meant to be.

// WHAT "FORBIDDEN FRUIT" IN YOUR LIFE IS CAUSING DISCONNECTION IN YOUR RELATIONSHIP WITH GOD?

Our story may not have had the start God intended, but it will have the ending His story deserves. Because God loved His children so much, He wanted nothing more than to make it right. That's where Jesus comes in and wipes the slate clean. All of the pain, bad choices, and shame will be gone someday. When Adam and Eve broke the original plan that led to death, Jesus put it back on course, promising us life.

// LOOK UP AND WRITE OUT 1 CORINTHIANS 15:22.

God had a redemptive plan from the very beginning, and someday we will be reunited with God forevermore, just the way it was meant to be! Even when the story first began, God had all of us in mind. This Christmas story, the story of God, is **For All.**

DOER OF THE WORD

How can you apply what you have learned from the Lord today?

_____

_____

_____

_____

SOCIAL CHALLENGE

// **WHAT IS SOMETHING YOU CAN SHARE ABOUT TODAY?**

// **STOP AND ASK GOD TO SHOW YOU WHO TO SHARE THIS WITH TODAY.**

// **WHO SHOULD YOU SHARE THIS WITH? (FINISH SENTENCE BELOW.)**

THIS MESSAGE IS *FOR ALL* BUT IT IS ALSO FOR:

// **PRAY OVER THAT PERSON(S) OR GROUP AND ASK GOD FOR AN OPPORTUNITY AND COURAGE TO SHARE.**

IF YOU SHARE ON SOCIAL MEDIA
BE SURE TO USE #SACREDHOLIDAYS + TAG @SACREDHOLIDAYS.

PROPHECIES

By Sharon Miller

TALK TO GOD

PRAISE // **REPENT** // **ASK** // **YIELD** // **STOP & LISTEN**

When I was a little girl, my family attended a traditional Presbyterian church in a towering gothic sanctuary. The floor and ceiling were lined with stone, which amplified a thunderous choir. Light streamed through stained glass windows and danced across pews, while we stood up and sat down, and stood up and sat down, reciting the church's liturgy.

As a child, there was a lot I didn't yet understand about church. I didn't understand what we were reading. I didn't understand what we were singing. I didn't understand the robes or the rhythms, and I certainly didn't understand Advent. One December morning, I remember standing on a stool behind a large mahogany pulpit, reading a passage from the Old Testament. I stretched my body to peer over the top, while my lips fumbled through the shape of words like "Bethlehem Ephrathah."

As a 10 year-old, I stared out at the congregation and wondered: *what does ANY of this have to do with baby Jesus?*

// **DO YOU HAVE SIMILAR CHILDHOOD MEMORIES? DESCRIBE BELOW.**

What I didn't understand at the time, is that Old Testament prophecies are a central part of the Christmas story. Jesus fulfilled over 300 Old Testament prophecies, and they teach us a great deal about who He was and why He came. They also point to the unity of Scripture—that there is no "Old Testament God" or "New Testament God"—but ONE God who is the same yesterday, today, and tomorrow.

What is especially remarkable about the Old Testament prophecies is how early they appear. The first prophecy of Jesus shows up in the very first pages of the Bible: Genesis 3. This chapter contains a prophecy known as the "protoevangelion" or "original gospel," because it is the very first hint of God's rescue plan for the world. We find it in verse 15, where God addresses the serpent, condemning him.

// **WRITE DOWN GENESIS 3:15.**

It would be easy to read this statement as a blanket rejection of snakes. Because who likes snakes? But God had a larger vision in view. The "offspring" is a reference to Adam and Eve's descendants, and one descendant in particular: Jesus Christ. Jesus is the offspring who will "crush the serpent's head," once and for all. Until that day, Satan will indeed get some bites. He will "strike our heels" with pain, suffering, sin, and shame, but these are merely flesh wounds with no lasting power. They will not change the end of the story.

It is breathtaking to consider what it means. Thousands of years before Jesus's birth, God was already pointing to His coming. As soon as our relationship with God was broken, He was already orchestrating its healing. This passage is the first glimpse of that good news.

In 2005, a contemplative nun named Sister Grace Remington drew an image of this prophecy. She titled it "Virgin Mary Consoles Eve," and in it, a downcast Eve faces a pregnant Mary, her shoulders hunched over in shame. Around Eve's leg is wrapped a serpent. Her right hand clutches an apple, while her left rests on Mary's swollen belly. Mary, in turn, looks tenderly at Eve, her hand touching Eve's distressed cheek. Under Mary's foot, the head of the serpent.

This image is a picture of the prophecy and its fulfillment, but it captures something grander as well: the arc of human history. It depicts God's redemptive master plan, and our own role in that plan. Each of us is Eve, and each of us is Mary. Each of us is condemned, and each of us is redeemed. Each of us is defeated, and each of us has overcome. We are bitten, but not destroyed.

In that sense, this prophecy is not simply about Jesus, but about all of us who trust in Him. The God who had a rescue plan is still rescuing us today. The God who fulfilled His promises is still trustworthy today. That is why the Old Testament prophecies matter. Not only do they validate the significance of Jesus's birth, but they tell a bigger story. Since the beginning of time, God has had this whole thing in the works, and we are a part of it.

// GENESIS 3 IS ONLY THE FIRST OF MANY PROPHECIES. READ ISAIAH 9:6-7 AND WRITE BELOW THE NAMES JESUS IS GIVEN.

How incredible it is to think, approximately 700 years prior to our Savior's birth, the glory of Jesus was already on display. The character, humanity, deity, everlastingness, authority, and provision of our coming King was already being talked about in homes and on the road, generation after generation! As objects of God's redemptive love, let's keep the momentum going by telling others about His saving grace.

DOER OF THE WORD

How can you apply what you have learned from the Lord today?

_____

_____

_____

_____

SOCIAL CHALLENGE

// **WHAT IS SOMETHING YOU CAN SHARE ABOUT TODAY?**

// **STOP AND ASK GOD TO SHOW YOU WHO TO SHARE THIS WITH TODAY.**

// **WHO SHOULD YOU SHARE THIS WITH? (FINISH SENTENCE BELOW.)**

THIS MESSAGE IS *FOR ALL* BUT IT IS ALSO FOR:

// **PRAY OVER THAT PERSON(S) OR GROUP AND ASK GOD FOR AN OPPORTUNITY AND COURAGE TO SHARE.**

IF YOU SHARE ON SOCIAL MEDIA
BE SURE TO USE #SACREDHOLIDAYS + TAG @SACREDHOLIDAYS.

ZECHARIAH

By Mandy Arioto

TALK TO GOD

PRAISE // REPENT // ASK // YIELD // STOP & LISTEN

Zechariah is the very first person mentioned in the Christmas story but often the last to be remembered. He was a priest in the division of Abijah, one of the 24 priestly details. Once a year, Zechariah and four of the other priests in his division were chosen to travel to Jerusalem to serve in the temple for one week before returning to their families. Their work included burning incense, offering sacrifices, and casting lots to determine which of the five priests would be chosen by God to perform the most important duty—to enter the temple, light the incense at the high altar, and emerge with a blessing for the people who had gathered for the holy occasion.

The lots are cast and Zechariah's name is drawn; he can hardly believe it. It is the honor of his life, and most priests never get chosen to serve at the temple, let alone enter the Holy place. His hands tremble as he offers sacrifices to make himself clean in the presence of God. Then taking a breath, he steps foot into God's home on earth. He is alone, lighting incense and chanting prayers under his breath when he suddenly realizes that he is no longer by himself.

// **READ LUKE 1:13-17. PUT YOURSELF IN ZECHARIAH'S SHOES. WOULD YOU FEEL HONORED? CURIOUS? OR JUST PLAIN SCARED?**

For Zechariah, terror swept over him. (Which is the curse of the professionally religious, we are often terrified when God interrupts our routine.) It isn't another priest who has suddenly joined him unceremoniously. Instead, it is a holy messenger, the angel Gabriel, who says what all angels say when humans discover their presence, "Do not fear." Then this messenger of God goes on to relay the news that Zechariah has been hoping to hear for decades, but which has become all but impossible at his age. He is going to have a son, but not just a son, a son who will be the announcer of the long-awaited Messiah.

// **REREAD LUKE 1:13 AND 17. THE ANSWER TO ZECHARIAH'S PRAYER FOR A SON WAS ANSWERED AT THE SAME TIME AS THE NATION'S PRAYER FOR THE MESSIAH. HOW CAN YOU, LIKE ZECHARIAH'S SON, GROW INTO A PERSON WHO POINTS PEOPLE TO JESUS?**

Zechariah and his wife Elizabeth are holy and honorable people who have prayed since their youth for a child, only to be met with disappointment month after month, and year after year. She has been labeled with the status of barren, a title that is grounds for Zechariah to divorce her, but he refuses. Instead, he lives with low-grade disappointment tinged with doubtful prayers that God might intervene, if not for him, for his wife who bears the brunt of hurtful comments and pity from neighbors who wonder what she has done to be cursed with the status of barren.

But here, in the temple of God, Zechariah hears the news he has been longing to hear. He and Elizabeth are going to be parents, and they are to name their son John, a name which no one in their family is named, which is very out of the ordinary in that day.

// **THE NAME OF ZECHARIAH'S SON WAS CHOSEN BY GOD—AND SO WAS GOD'S SON, JESUS. JOHN MEANS "THE LORD IS GRACIOUS," AND JESUS MEANS "THE LORD SAVES." WRITE A SIMPLE PRAYER, THANKING GOD FOR GRACIOUSLY SAVING YOU.**

Zechariah can't believe it, and he says so. Which is the last thing he says, because after that, the angel strikes him mute. He can't talk—which may be the greatest gift he has ever experienced. Because while Elizabeth was the one with the title of barren, it has been suggested that the person who really holds that title in this story is Zechariah. The commentaries say it was his sin of disbelief that caused the angel to clam him up, but I am more inclined to label it a habit of hopelessness, one with a barren soul, void of faith and far too comfortable with disappointment.

Zechariah emerges from the temple where people have gathered to receive the customary blessing of the priest leaving the temple. But there are no words, only a one-sided game of charades because no one can guess what happened inside. So Zechariah goes home, and although he can't talk, he can do other things, and his wife Elizabeth conceives a child in her old age.

A similar story of an unlikely and unexpected pregnancy is happening simultaneously, to a beloved niece of Elizabeth's named Mary. Mary comes to visit Elizabeth during her pregnancy, and the story of Christmas bubbles up in both their wombs, although neither have any clue that the hope of the world is growing under their ribs. Mary stays with Elizabeth for six months and is welcome company since Elizabeth's husband can't say a word. He is undergoing a mandatory sabbatical, a gestation period of his own, where his commanded silence is preparing the way for hope to be birthed.

Sometimes silence is the best thing that could ever happen to us. We are bombarded by words. Very few of them come at us without an agenda, promising things they cannot deliver, arguing a point or stealing our attention, which is exactly why silence is so hard to deal with, but often the very thing that can restore our hopelessness.

Yet isn't it in silence that we're able to make room for reverence? We leave things unsaid in order to refocus our attention on the hope-filled mystery of God who hears our prayers and fulfills his promises.

DESCRIBE A TIME OF SILENCE, WHETHER DUE TO ILLNESS OR INJURY, OR SIMPLY DURING A QUIET TIME WITH GOD, WHEN YOU WERE ABLE TO FOCUS ON YOUR SAVIOR LIKE NEVER BEFORE.

Nine months after Zechariah's encounter in the temple, Elizabeth gives birth to a son. At his circumcision, the family is gathered wondering what family name Zechariah will speak over him, but instead, he writes it down: John. With that declaration, Zechariah's mouth is opened, and he begins praising God for His faithfulness. It is in silence that hope is restored and prayers are fulfilled.

Zechariah is the patron saint of advent, the season of practicing patience and waiting. Perhaps the one way to quiet our doubt and fear in this season of anticipation, is to make peace with involuntary silence. May the experience of Zechariah remind us that silence and waiting are not a curse, they are an essential part of a story that has an outcome that might seem impossible at the moment, but just ahead is a long awaited surprise where God does something remarkably unexpected in our lives and the world.

Which is a perfect message to start off the Christmas season as you are going through your everyday life, praying for what you need the Lord to do. And as you continue to serve Him by following His instruction, Yahweh will remember your prayers before Him, and will fulfill His covenant with kindness just as He did with the birth of John the Baptist. Zechariah wanted a son; God linked him through that son to the story of Jesus the Messiah forever. We have a God who outdoes Himself in remembering our longings and being faithful to His promises **For All.**

That is a Christmas miracle if I ever heard one.

DOER OF THE WORD

How can you apply what you have learned from the Lord today?

SOCIAL CHALLENGE

// **WHAT IS SOMETHING YOU CAN SHARE ABOUT TODAY?**

// **STOP AND ASK GOD TO SHOW YOU WHO TO SHARE THIS WITH TODAY.**

// **WHO SHOULD YOU SHARE THIS WITH? (FINISH SENTENCE BELOW.)**

THIS MESSAGE IS *FOR ALL* BUT IT IS ALSO FOR:

// **PRAY OVER THAT PERSON(S) OR GROUP AND ASK GOD FOR AN OPPORTUNITY AND COURAGE TO SHARE.**

IF YOU SHARE ON SOCIAL MEDIA
BE SURE TO USE #SACREDHOLIDAYS + TAG @SACREDHOLIDAYS.

GENEALOGY

By Elizabeth Hyndman

TALK TO GOD

PRAISE // **REPENT** // **ASK** // **YIELD** // **STOP & LISTEN**

The genealogies show us promises fulfilled. They show us our hope will not be dismayed. They show us God's sovereignty, loving kindness, and wisdom.

We tend to want to skip over the genealogies in the Bible. They're lists of unfamiliar and difficult-to-pronounce names. We skim through, moving quickly onto what we consider the main plot of the story. Today, we're not skipping.

// **READ MATTHEW 1:1-17.**

Most likely, you saw a lot of names you'd never heard before. (Personally, I think this would be a great place to find your next pet's name. There probably aren't a lot of other Zerubbabels at the dog park.) Also likely, you saw some names you recognized. Perhaps you even know some of the people listed fairly well.

// **JOT DOWN THE NAMES YOU RECOGNIZE FROM THIS LIST.**

While we may be familiar with a few names on this list, Matthew's original audience was familiar with many more. Matthew wrote to people who were a part of this family. They had heard of Abraham, Isaac, and Jacob since they were born. Ruth and Rahab were probably familiar stories. They knew of Jehoshaphat and Amminadab like we know of Benjamin Franklin, Princess Diana, or Great-Aunt Ethel whose chocolate fudge pie recipe is a family legend.

They also knew of the promises each of these people held in their hearts. From Genesis 3:15, when God promised Eve an offspring to crush the serpent's head, God's people had been waiting on the snake-crusher.

Matthew's genealogy begins with a different promise, though. He begins in verse 2 with Abraham.

// **READ GENESIS 12:1-3. WHAT DID GOD PROMISE ABRAHAM (THEN KNOWN AS ABRAM)?**

Only a few chapters (though many years) after God promised to bring a serpent-crusher through Eve, He promised to make Abraham into a great nation.

If you know anything about Abraham's story, you know this was impossible without God. But Abraham believed. And Abraham died before the promise was fulfilled.

We don't have time to go through every name on this family tree, but this first stanza alone (verses 2-6) has some incredible stories. Jacob stole an inheritance, Judah sold his brother into slavery and fathered Perez through, let's just say, a not-so-traditional relationship with Tamar. Boaz, Rahab's son, married Ruth as her kinsman redeemer and had King David's grandfather, Obed.

Then we get to King David.

// **READ 2 SAMUEL 7:8-9,15. WHAT DID GOD PROMISE DAVID?**

Here's another promise impossible without God: He promises to establish David's kingdom forever. David believed and David died without seeing that promise fulfilled.

Then the rest of these names? They carried on these promises. They remembered, they taught them to their children, they worshiped the "God of Abraham and Isaac and Jacob." And they died, too, without seeing these promises fulfilled. Until we get to verse 16.

// **READ VERSE 16 AGAIN. WHAT NAME IS USED FOR JESUS IN THIS VERSE?**

The name of Christ is synonymous with Messiah, the King. This genealogy you just read, this list of names, it is the ancestry of the Promised One, the King of kings. Mary is the only person on this list who we know lived to see her Son, the Christ, conquer death and crush the head of the serpent. But what about the other promises? Did Abraham's family become a great nation? Is David's family still on the throne?

// **READ ROMANS 8:14-17. FOR THOSE OF US IN CHRIST, WHO DOES THIS VERSE SAY WE ARE?**

We have been adopted into the family of God. We are God's children, coheirs with Christ! That means that this genealogy, this list of begats and fathereds, is our list too. This is our family tree.

// **WHAT DOES OUR ADOPTION MEAN FOR ABRAHAM'S FAMILY LINE?**

That's why we can confidently sing, "Many sons had Father Abraham. I am one of them!" In Genesis 15, God says to Abraham, "'Look at the sky and count the stars, if you are able to count them.' Then he said to him, 'Your offspring will be that numerous'" (CSB).

// **READ ACTS 2:29-36. WHAT DO THESE VERSES SAY ABOUT DAVID?**

// **WHAT TWO NAMES DO THESE VERSES GIVE TO JESUS?**

Jesus is Lord and Messiah. He is the King and Ruler. In Jesus, we see the promise to David fulfilled. David's descendant still sits on the throne and will reign forever.

Matthew's original audience would have been familiar with the names on this list and they would have been familiar with the promises given. Matthew is establishing the foundation upon which he will tell the story of the Messiah, the Promised One, the One who came to be our Savior and Lord.

// **LOOK BACK AT THE FAMILIAR NAMES YOU LISTED AFTER FIRST READING THE GENEALOGIES. WHAT DO YOU KNOW ABOUT THOSE PEOPLE? (YOU MAY HAVE MORE INFORMATION ON SOME THAN OTHERS.)**

// **WHAT ABOUT THE INCLUSION OF THESE NAMES IN JESUS'S FAMILY TREE GIVES YOU HOPE?**

When we look at the genealogies, we can see God's divine hand at work among the women, the Gentiles, the kings, the thieves, the adulterers, the warriors, and the faithful. God worked in the lives of these very broken men and women to establish His eternal family line and bring about the fulfillment to the promises He made.

The truth is, there are still some promises we're waiting on. We're waiting for Jesus to come again and establish His eternal throne. We're waiting on our inheritance. We're waiting to see how He works all things for our good and His glory. In the waiting, though, we can look back and see what He's already done. We can remember how He was faithful to the people on this list, the people in our family. We can remember how He has been faithful **For All,** and we can trust that He will be faithful forever.

// **WRITE A PRAYER OF REMEMBRANCE AND THANKSGIVING. REMEMBER THE WAYS GOD HAS BEEN FAITHFUL TO HIS PROMISES IN THE PAST AND HOW HE HAS BEEN FAITHFUL TO YOU. THANK HIM FOR JESUS, THE SERPENT-CRUSHER, THE KING OF KINGS. THANK HIM FOR HOPE THAT WILL NOT BE DISMAYED.**

"Now to the King eternal, immortal, invisible, the only God, be honor and glory forever and ever. Amen" (1 Timothy 1:17, CSB).

DOER OF THE WORD

How can you apply what you have learned from the Lord today?

SOCIAL CHALLENGE

// **WHAT IS SOMETHING YOU CAN SHARE ABOUT TODAY?**

// **STOP AND ASK GOD TO SHOW YOU WHO TO SHARE THIS WITH TODAY.**

// **WHO SHOULD YOU SHARE THIS WITH? (FINISH SENTENCE BELOW.)**

THIS MESSAGE IS *FOR ALL* BUT IT IS ALSO FOR:

// **PRAY OVER THAT PERSON(S) OR GROUP AND ASK GOD FOR AN OPPORTUNITY AND COURAGE TO SHARE.**

IF YOU SHARE ON SOCIAL MEDIA
BE SURE TO USE #SACREDHOLIDAYS + TAG @SACREDHOLIDAYS.

MARY

By Jandi Harris

TALK TO GOD

PRAISE // REPENT // ASK // YIELD // STOP & LISTEN

With tears streaming down my face and my hands stretched high above my head, I belted out the words, "Your love never fails it never gives up, it never runs out on me. It goes on and on and on . . . " Nevermind the fact that the concert was officially over and people in the arena were pushing past me to get to the nearest exit. I noticed an elderly woman staring back at me and whispering to her younger companion. Maybe I was too loud? Too off-key? I didn't know, but I continued to worship anyway. Within a few moments, a lady was standing in front of me, reaching out a closed fist. I was a bit confused and concerned, but I reached out my hand to accept whatever was in her hands. She smiled and emptied her outstretched hand into mine. A few seconds later, I opened my hand to find several crumpled twenty-dollar bills and a five dollar bill. I was surprised and in awe all at once because I had never before experienced such an encounter.

You see, about three weeks prior, I felt God calling me to attend a conference that would better equip me to do what God was putting on my heart, but I did not have enough money on hand to even reserve a space. And honestly, I was not confident that it would come to pass. This encounter reminded me that God not only designs specific encounters to prepare us for His assignments and His call, but that He fully equips us to carry out His purposes.

The announcement of the birth of Jesus to Mary is a specific encounter which prepared Mary for her assignment, giving birth to our Lord and Savior Jesus Christ, the Promise of Hope to all of mankind.

// READ LUKE 1:26-33 AND SUMMARIZE WHAT HAPPENED.

God sent the angel Gabriel with a unique message to a distinct region, in a specific city, at a particular time, and to a special person. It was intended for Mary—and Mary alone. This encounter was not haphazard, and today, God still longs for encounters designed just for us, with special instructions just for us. If we are not careful, we can miss those God encounters and view them as interruptions. We are all guilty of sometimes only wanting God when we want Him and according to our expectations. But most times, God does not fit our convenient timelines or give blessings in neat and perfect packages.

// CAN YOU THINK OF OTHER TIMES IN THE BIBLE WHEN GOD DID SOMETHING AT, OR WHAT MIGHT HAVE SEEMED LIKE, AN UNUSUAL TIME OR IN AN ATYPICAL WAY?

// WHAT ABOUT IN YOUR LIFE? HAVE YOU EXPERIENCED GOD DOING THINGS OUTSIDE THE NORM?

God always gives us reassurance when He calls us to do something for Him.

// WRITE OUT SOME OF THE THINGS THE ANGEL SAID ABOUT MARY IN LUKE 1:28-30.

God knows that our hearts are often weighed down with fear and uncertainty because we focus on what we can physically see, all the while He desires for us to see ourselves as He sees us. He desires that we keep our God-identity in the forefront. Before Mary ever received instructions from the angel of the Lord, she was reminded of how God saw her—favored and with Him.

Even though Mary received reassurance of her identity, she was still troubled and uncertain. The angel reminded Mary not to fear. From this we can know that in our season or assignment we don't have to fear because we know He is in control. Though you do not have all the answers, do not fear. As for Mary, the Lord had already equipped her to complete her assignment. He needed her to know it, to believe it, and to not question or doubt it.

// THINK ABOUT WHERE YOU ARE RIGHT NOW IN LIFE, WHERE GOD MIGHT BE LEADING YOU. WHAT ARE YOUR CONCERNS ABOUT THIS SEASON OR ASSIGNMENT HE HAS PLACED BEFORE YOU?

Mary's assignment was much bigger than she was capable of fulfilling on her own. She would carry and birth the Savior of the world, the Son of the Most High, the King whose kingdom will never end. A big assignment indeed! Maybe she felt like the job was too big for her. Maybe she felt unqualified, ill-equipped, and not worthy of this call. Maybe, like you and I often feel, she felt as though she did not have life together and that someone else would be a better fit for this assignment. Maybe she felt the timing was not right. But God knew she was worthy. God knew she was already prepared and equipped for the assignment. God knew the time was perfect for birth to be given to a promise that would change the world forever. Mary's encounter with the Holy Spirit led to the birth of our Savior, Jesus Christ, who came *For All.*

Such God encounters remind us that, like Mary, we carry a promise inside of us that is greater than the world around us.

// **WHAT DO YOU LEARN ABOUT JESUS FROM WHAT THE ANGEL TOLD MARY IN LUKE 1:31-33.**

// **WHICH OF THESE ASPECT(S) OF CHRIST'S IDENTITY DO YOU NEED TO HOLD FAST TO RIGHT NOW?**

Rejoice, highly favored one! Where there is instruction from God, there is provision. Rejoice, for He will surely complete His work. Rejoice, our Savior reigns on the throne of God and He will reign forever and *For All.*

DOER OF THE WORD

How can you apply what you have learned from the Lord today?

SOCIAL CHALLENGE

// **WHAT IS SOMETHING YOU CAN SHARE ABOUT TODAY?**

// **STOP AND ASK GOD TO SHOW YOU WHO TO SHARE THIS WITH TODAY.**

// **WHO SHOULD YOU SHARE THIS WITH? (FINISH SENTENCE BELOW.)**

THIS MESSAGE IS *FOR ALL* BUT IT IS ALSO FOR:

// **PRAY OVER THAT PERSON(S) OR GROUP AND ASK GOD FOR AN OPPORTUNITY AND COURAGE TO SHARE.**

IF YOU SHARE ON SOCIAL MEDIA
BE SURE TO USE #SACREDHOLIDAYS + TAG @SACREDHOLIDAYS.

JOSEPH

By Christina Crenshaw

TALK TO GOD

PRAISE // REPENT // ASK // YIELD // STOP & LISTEN

READ MATTHEW 1:18-24 AND LUKE 1:27 AND RECORD SOME OF THE DETAILS BELOW.

An Angel of the Lord spoke to Joseph in a dream and affirmed what Mary had heard: Joseph would become a father through the most supernatural of circumstances. Joseph chose to trust and obey the Lord by taking Mary as his wife and accepting Jesus as his son.

SHARE ABOUT A TIME OR SEASON OF LIFE THAT HAS REQUIRED GREAT FAITH AND TRUST IN THE LORD.

WHAT WERE A FEW BIBLICAL, UNSHAKEABLE PROMISES, AFFIRMATIONS, OR FULFILLMENTS THE LORD SPOKE TO YOU DURING THAT TIME?

There was a lengthy season of life when I frequently thought of Jesus's parents, young Joseph and Mary. For four long, difficult, and painful years, my husband and I struggled to conceive. In those years, we subjected ourselves to a battery of tests, surgeries, and infertility treatments. Doctors could not find anything wrong with us, but they were also unable to determine why we could not conceive. "Unexplained Infertility" was the official diagnosis. And when we finally did conceive, with a great deal of medical assistance, sadly, we miscarried six weeks into the pregnancy. The road to motherhood was a heartbreaking experience. And though the pilgrimage occurred over five years ago, tears flow easily and a hard lump rises in my throat whenever I think back on those years of trial. But even in that bitter taste of trial, there was also a sweet, deep intimacy that emerged from a place of knowing and trusting the Lord. Through the cloud of unknowing, I trusted His goodness.

It was in that time of infertility I thought of Jesus's parents. Joseph and Mary—who conceived without trying, who had not planned to parent so early in their marriage, who likely suffered great humiliation in their small town, and who trusted the Lord even when their family planning was beyond their control. I greatly admired their faith. And I especially admired Joseph's resolve to trust the Lord amidst the unknown.

Little is known about Joseph of Nazareth, husband to Mary and earthly father to Jesus Christ. In fact, his name is mentioned directly only three times in Scripture: twice in the birth narratives (Matthew 1-2; Luke 1-2), and once in reference to genealogy (Luke 3:23).

What little we do know about Joseph solidifies three essential truths that support the Biblical narrative of salvation. First, Joseph is a descendant of the House of King David (Luke 2:4). Second, even if not his biological father, Joseph was chosen to parent Jesus (Matthew 1:22-25). Third, the Lord had Joseph's heart and therefore knew he was trustworthy. Joseph hailed from royalty, was selected to raise humanity's Savior, and trusted the Lord even when he doubted his role in the fulfillment of Scripture. Joseph was a man of character. Scripture calls him righteous and compassionate (Matthew 1:19). It also states he was a man who loved God's laws (Matthew 1:24). So it is not hard to imagine why Joseph would obey the Lord and choose Mary as his wife, even given her inexplicable conception. It is also not difficult to see how Joseph embraced his role in the salvation narrative, even if he didn't fully understand it.

There are several Old Testament verses that prophesy the life of Christ and His genealogy hailing from the House of David.

// **READ AND WRITE OUT OR SUMMARIZE ISAIAH 7:14.**

// **READ AND WRITE OUT OR SUMMARIZE ISAIAH 9:6-7.**

// READ AND WRITE OUT OR SUMMARIZE PSALM 72:10-11.

// READ AND WRITE OUT OR SUMMARIZE JEREMIAH 23:5.

Now that the prophecy is fulfilled, it is apparent how God wove the Biblical narrative of Jesus's birth, life, crucifixion, and resurrection throughout the Bible For All to know.

// HOW MIGHT IT HAVE BEEN EASY FOR JOSEPH TO CONNECT OLD TESTAMENT PROPHECY TO WHAT THE ANGEL OF THE LORD SPOKE TO HIM? BUT HOW MIGHT IT ALSO HAVE BEEN DIFFICULT FOR JOSEPH TO BELIEVE HE WAS CHOSEN TO FULFILL THE BIBLICAL PROMISES?

I cannot say with complete confidence I knew God was calling me to motherhood during my season of infertility struggles. There was no word of affirmation from an angel. There was no burning bush. There was no voice from the heavens. Rather, I simply leaned into the longing of my heart. I trusted the Lord's word that we are all called to be fruitful and multiply, whether biologically and/or spiritually. And so I fought against the lies of the one who comes to steal, kill, and destroy our hope, faith, and joy.

After several years of fertility treatments and a miscarriage, we finally conceived and welcomed our first born, Christopher, into our family. We were elated! Years of hope deferred had made our hearts sick, but it had not caused us to turn or harden our hearts to the Lord. We trusted Him. And we were overjoyed by the fulfillment of our longing, and we praised God for him.

Doctors told us we had less than a one-percent chance of conceiving on our own based upon the statistics of how many years we'd been trying. But we had learned in our journey to trust the Lord and not lean on our own understanding, or purely the doctor's statistics, when we looked to the future. You can imagine our joy when what I thought was a case of flu was actually the first weeks of pregnancy with my second son, Corban, who was conceived without medical assistance. We named him Corban, "a gift dedicated unto the Lord," because our journey to parenthood taught us our heart was the gift the Lord was after all along.

"The eyes of the LORD range throughout the earth to strengthen those whose hearts are fully committed to him" (2 Chronicles 16:9). We serve a God who desires the intimacy of our heart, who can be trusted to fulfill His promises—in His timing and in accordance to His will.

// WHAT ARE YOU TRUSTING THE LORD FOR RIGHT NOW? THINK ON THE LORD'S FAITHFULNESS TO JOSEPH AND MARY. THINK ON HOW THE LORD WOVE JESUS INTO KING DAVID'S LINEAGE, A MAN WHO WAS AFTER GOD'S HEART (ACTS 13:22). HOW DO YOU KNOW, WITHOUT DOUBT, THE LORD IS FOR YOU AND HAS A PERFECT PLAN?

DOER OF THE WORD

How can you apply what you have learned from the Lord today?

SOCIAL CHALLENGE

// **WHAT IS SOMETHING YOU CAN SHARE ABOUT TODAY?**

// **STOP AND ASK GOD TO SHOW YOU WHO TO SHARE THIS WITH TODAY.**

// **WHO SHOULD YOU SHARE THIS WITH? (FINISH SENTENCE BELOW.)**

THIS MESSAGE IS *FOR ALL* BUT IT IS ALSO FOR:

// **PRAY OVER THAT PERSON(S) OR GROUP AND ASK GOD FOR AN OPPORTUNITY AND COURAGE TO SHARE.**

IF YOU SHARE ON SOCIAL MEDIA
BE SURE TO USE #SACREDHOLIDAYS + TAG @SACREDHOLIDAYS.

THE HOLY SPIRIT

By Amber Burger

TALK TO GOD

PRAISE // REPENT // ASK // YIELD // STOP & LISTEN

_____

_____

_____

_____

Because the story of Christmas is such a fascinating narrative with so many plot lines to follow, the Holy Spirit often gets skimmed over. As Christians, the part the Holy Spirit plays in the story of Jesus's birth is so huge that it is the very reality that sets Jesus apart from all other men. So, to help us better see how He is moving in and through us this holiday season, let's draw the attention of our minds and affection of our hearts toward the beautiful role the Holy Spirit plays in the Nativity story.

// **READ MATTHEW 1:18-25.**

// **WHAT ROLE DID THE HOLY SPIRIT PLAY IN THE BIRTH STORY OF JESUS?**

// WHAT ROLE DOES MAN (JOSEPH) PLAY IN THE CONCEPTION OF JESUS?

// HOW DOES THAT MAKE JESUS DIFFERENT FROM ALL OTHER HUMANS?

// WHAT DOES THIS KNOWLEDGE TELL YOU ABOUT THE CHARACTER OF THE HOLY SPIRIT?

Jesus, in human form, was not conceived by man, but by the Holy Spirit! What a beautiful mystery! The Holy Spirit is creative! The Holy Spirit cares deeply about the salvation of those on earth and uses His creativity to be a part in Jesus's human conception.

It is easy for us, because of our fear of "the mystery" and the elusive nature of many teachings we come across, to stay focused on the role of the Father and of Jesus in the restoration narrative throughout Scripture.

// DOES THIS RESONATE WITH YOU? DO YOU FIND YOURSELF FOCUSING ON THE ROLE OF THE FATHER AND OF JESUS OVER THAT OF THE HOLY SPIRIT? IF SO, WHY DO YOU THINK THIS IS?

When we do this, we miss the role of the Holy Spirit all together. My hope for you this season is that you will set aside those fears and open your heart and mind to hear and see the Holy Spirit's character ministering to you everyday. After all, without the Holy Spirit's role in the Christmas story, we could not count on the salvation Jesus offers—which is not a minor miss!

Beyond the Holy Spirit's role in the conception of Jesus into human form, let's explore a little more and find some amazing characteristics of the Holy Spirit throughout the Christmas narrative.

As we read the story of Mary becoming pregnant before she was married to Joseph, we empathize with her as we know in her culture she would have been marginalized, shunned, and blasphemed for such a thing. We see the Holy Spirit advocating and encouraging her every step of the way. From the sweet time with her beloved friend Elizabeth, to the angel appearing on her behalf to Joseph in order to explain her situation (Matthew 1:18-22), the Holy

Spirit went ahead of her and advocated not only for the child in her womb, but for Mary's very heart. Where God could have given her the task to carry the Son of God, leaving her to fend for herself, He chose instead, in His kindness, to meet her in her fears, comfort her heart, and advocate for her along the way.

// **LET'S FIRST LOOK AT MARY'S VISIT WITH ELIZABETH IN LUKE 1:39-41. WHAT HAPPENED TO ELIZABETH AT THE SOUND OF MARY'S GREETING?**

// **NOW READ LUKE 1:42-45. IN VERSE 44, FOR WHAT REASON DID THE BABY LEAP? WHAT DOES THIS TELL YOU ABOUT THE HOLY SPIRIT?**

Not only is the Holy Spirit the giver of great joy (Galatians 5:22, Acts 13:52), but He is our Advocate, Helper, and Comforter.

// **READ JESUS'S PROMISE TO SEND THE HOLY SPIRIT IN JOHN 14:15-30 IN THE AMPLIFIED BIBLE.**

We see Him as our Advocate. The Holy Spirit is for us. He advocates on our behalf to the Father and opens our minds and hearts to the ways of the Father. We even see Jesus Himself leaning into the advocacy of the Spirit in the wilderness in Matthew 4.

We see Him as our Helper. As it came time for Jesus to leave earth, He tells His disciples not to let their "hearts be troubled" (John 14:1). A few thoughts later He promises to send them a Helper, One who will teach, guide, and leave them with peace.

We see Him as our Comforter. When you feel like you are alone, you don't fit in, you are unsure of the path ahead, and life is chaotic, we have a Great Advocate within us! We have a Comforter and Counselor, ready and willing to comfort and guide us. The Holy Spirit fills us, the new temple, as we follow and listen to His leading.

// NOW TAKE TIME TO LIST THE MOMENTS YOU'VE KNOWN HIM AS YOUR ADVOCATE, HELPER, AND COMFORTER.

This holiday season, take a moment to ask the Holy Spirit to well up in your heart. Ask Him for eyes to see and ears to hear for the Kingdom. Ask Him to help you see how He has gone ahead of you and advocated on your behalf. Thank Him for the hope of His presence and for not leaving you alone when He left this earth.

DOER OF THE WORD

How can you apply what you have learned from the Lord today?

_____

_____

_____

_____

SOCIAL CHALLENGE

// WHAT IS SOMETHING YOU CAN SHARE ABOUT TODAY?

// STOP AND ASK GOD TO SHOW YOU WHO TO SHARE THIS WITH TODAY.

// WHO SHOULD YOU SHARE THIS WITH? (FINISH SENTENCE BELOW.)

THIS MESSAGE IS _FOR ALL_ BUT IT IS ALSO FOR:

// PRAY OVER THAT PERSON(S) OR GROUP AND ASK GOD FOR AN OPPORTUNITY AND COURAGE TO SHARE.

IF YOU SHARE ON SOCIAL MEDIA
BE SURE TO USE #SACREDHOLIDAYS + TAG @SACREDHOLIDAYS.

ELIZABETH

By Jenn Jett Barrett

TALK TO GOD

PRAISE // REPENT // ASK // YIELD // STOP & LISTEN

I listened to a dear friend teach from the first chapter of Luke a couple years ago, a time I had been wading through the unexpected journey of divorce at 39-years-old. You never think you will find yourself there, but there I was after 15 years of marriage. I was learning to accept that sometimes God allows the very thing He never intended for us—struggle and pain—to be the very thing that draws us to the gospel in ways we've never known before. And I remember thinking to myself: *I want to live my life like Elizabeth.*

// **READ LUKE 1:6-7. NOTICE HOW ELIZABETH WAS BARREN YET BLAMELESS.**

Scripture tells us early on in Luke that Elizabeth was old and barren, and when a woman is barren, the "public" assumption was that she was either unfaithful to God or unfaithful to her husband. But Luke is clear to let us know that "both of them were upright in the sight of God, observing all the Lord's commandments and regulations blamelessly." This does not mean they were sinless. Rather, they lived a life of obedience and divine worship. Can you imagine what that must have felt like, to live a life faithful to the Lord, yet seen as disgraceful to others? Even though Elizabeth was aware of what people were saying, she stayed the course and remained upright and blameless.

// WHEN WAS THE LAST TIME YOU FELT JUDGED BY OTHERS? HOW DID THAT MAKE YOU FEEL?

// NOW READ LUKE 1:23-25. NOTICE HOW ELIZABETH WAS BOASTFUL AND BELIEVED HER GOD.

I absolutely love what Elizabeth did right after she found out she was pregnant. Her response wasn't to erase the disgrace in public, her response was to BOAST in the Lord's work in seclusion. She BELIEVED He had done this, not luck or a medical miracle, but the Lord. It is a reminder that the Lord's merciless withholding can actually be His strategic timing. And John was to be born for such a time as this.

Luke 1:14-15a says, "He will be a joy and delight to you, and many will rejoice because of his birth, for he will be great in the sight of the Lord . . ." And Luke 1:16 says, "He will bring back many of the people of Israel to the Lord their God."

You see, John wasn't just born for the people, he was born for Mary and Jesus. Born for Mary in that, due to Elizabeth's own gossiped-about pregnancy, she understood the disgrace that comes from public shaming, which allowed Elizabeth to comfort Mary, helping to keep her young eyes fixed on the Lord. And born for Jesus in that God saw fit for the Son of man to have a friend.

// DO YOU HAVE FRIENDSHIPS THAT SEEM HANDPICKED FROM GOD? PLEASE SHARE IN THE SPACE BELOW.

// READ LUKE 1:39-45 AND NOTICE HOW ELIZABETH WAS COMPASSIONATE AMID THE BLESSING.

Mary starts off by recognizing that God is her Savior (Luke 1:47). Only sinners need a Savior. She knows that her life is full of sin, undeserving of this calling God has on her life.

Elizabeth was experiencing the blessing of a baby—her baby! She had waited who knows how long. Then, this young girl who isn't even married yet, rushes in to tell of her unexplainable news. I am moved by this next part: "When Elizabeth heard Mary's greeting, the baby leaped in her womb, and Elizabeth was filled with the Holy Spirit" (Luke 1:41). Decades of Elizabeth's deep devotion for the Lord is evidenced by being filled with the Holy Spirit AND coming to an understanding that this blessing is not about her, but about the Messiah who is to come. The Spirit of the Lord moved Elizabeth to compassion, joy, and celebration.

Luke 1:42-45 says, "In a loud voice she exclaimed: 'Blessed are you among women, and blessed is the child you will bear! But why am I so favored, that the mother of my Lord should come to me? As soon as the sound of your greeting reached my ears, the baby in my womb leaped for joy. Blessed is she who has believed that the Lord would fulfill his promises to her!'"

// WRITE DOWN THE LAST SENTENCE FROM THE SCRIPTURE ABOVE, REPLACING "SHE" WITH YOUR NAME. WHAT PROMISE ARE YOU CURRENTLY BELIEVING GOD FOR?

And then she asks the most profound why. It's not "why does Mary get to be the mother of my Lord?" Rather, "Why am I so favored that the mother of my Lord should come to me?"

Elizabeth's eyes stay fixed on the Lord and on His ways, His plans, and His timing, believing He is who He says He is: FAITHFUL. ALWAYS. Thus God used Elizabeth's disgraceful barrenness to experience the Gospel in a way she had never known.

DOER OF THE WORD

How can you apply what you have learned from the Lord today?

SOCIAL CHALLENGE

// **WHAT IS SOMETHING YOU CAN SHARE ABOUT TODAY?**

// **STOP AND ASK GOD TO SHOW YOU WHO TO SHARE THIS WITH TODAY.**

// **WHO SHOULD YOU SHARE THIS WITH? (FINISH SENTENCE BELOW.)**

THIS MESSAGE IS *FOR ALL* BUT IT IS ALSO FOR:

// **PRAY OVER THAT PERSON(S) OR GROUP AND ASK GOD FOR AN OPPORTUNITY AND COURAGE TO SHARE.**

IF YOU SHARE ON SOCIAL MEDIA
BE SURE TO USE #SACREDHOLIDAYS + TAG @SACREDHOLIDAYS.

MARY'S SONG

By Rebecca Renfrow

TALK TO GOD

PRAISE // REPENT // ASK // YIELD // STOP & LISTEN

If I ever get a tattoo, it will be the word "grace" written in beautiful script to serve as a daily reminder of God's unending grace. My hubby says I shouldn't get a tattoo because I change my mind more often than I change underwear. He might be right, but for some reason I don't think I will ever change my mind about how significant the word grace is to me.

I grew up in a broken home. Instead of a home filled with family dinners, parents cheering for their kids at all their sports events, and Christmas Eve nights spent around the tree, my home was filled with yelling, neglect, and selfish, toxic behavior.

But my life now is filled with so much of God's grace that I am sometimes stunned by its presence. I am reminded often of how God has taken this unworthy small town girl, born in a broken home filled with pain and heartache, and replanted her in a life filled with forgiveness, patience, love, and most of all, grace.

I met my husband in college. He was good, patient, kind, gentle, forgiving. He was all the things I didn't know men could really be, deep inside their core. He came with a loving, Christian family who not only accepted me in all my brokenness, but also loved me unconditionally, adopting me into their family and calling me "daughter" right from the beginning.

They introduced me to Jesus.

Grace.

Jesus did that for me. And He did that for you, too. He does it **For All.**

// HOW HAS GOD SHOWN HIS GRACE IN YOUR LIFE?

Earlier in this study, we read how the angel Gabriel came to Mary to tell her that the Lord had chosen her for a very special purpose—that she would give birth to the son of God. Like for real, y'all—an unmarried, teenage peasant girl who had just found out she was pregnant with the Messiah. Talk about being called to do something huge!

// THINK AGAIN OF HOW MARY MUST HAVE FELT IN THAT MOMENT, UPON FIRST HEARING THE NEWS. WRITE DOWN YOUR THOUGHTS.

I can just hear Mary thinking, *Who me? Are you serious God? How will this thing work? Who am I to do this for you and the world.* And then replying like she did in Luke 1:34, *How will this be, since I am still a virgin?*

Just a couple of years ago, God gave me a new task. He asked me to take my restored heart along with my story, and share His grace with women who don't know their worth in Jesus. He asked me to start a podcast and become a life and business coach focused on supporting women who have a strong desire to live out their passion—while still being the mom they crave to be. He also asked me to be open and honest about my personal struggles of feeling worthy enough to do His work. I immediately thought: *Who me? Are you serious God? The girl who struggles to know her own worth, to take her own advice when it comes to believing she is worthy because of all that Jesus has done for her? Who am I to do this for You?*

// WRITE DOWN LUKE 1:37. HOW DID GABRIEL RESPOND?

And there you have it, my friends. Nothing, not one single thing, is impossible with God. Nothing.

// HAS GOD EVER ASKED YOU TO DO SOMETHING THAT FEELS SO BIG AND SCARY THAT YOU IMMEDIATELY START SHAKING IN YOUR ANKLE BOOTS?

// WITH THAT CONTEXT, NOW READ LUKE 1:46-55 AND WRITE DOWN WHAT STANDS OUT TO YOU THE MOST.

Mary starts off by recognizing that God is her Savior (Luke 1:47). Only sinners need a Savior. She knows that her life is full of sin, undeserving of this calling God has on her life.

She then sings of God looking down on her humble state (Luke 1:48). Literally, Mary sees her littleness, both in the world's eyes and in God's. Her words tell us she felt unworthy to be chosen by God.

She sings that His mercy is from generation to generation on those who fear Him (Luke 1:50). That's Mary's poetic way of saying, "God, you didn't give me what I deserve. Instead, You gave me grace and showed me mercy, withholding what I deserve, just as you've done for generations past." Oh how grateful I am for that. It comes back to grace, lots and lots of grace. Thank you, Jesus!

In this first part of Mary's song, we see something wonderful and true about God: He loves the disqualified and the unimpressive. We are all unworthy of God's grace. But He gives it to us freely regardless. With grace He equips us to do big, important things for His kingdom.

Throughout the rest of her song, Mary sings of radical reversals for three groups of people. He will rescue the helpless (Luke 1:51), exalt the humble (Luke 1:52), and fill the hungry (Luke 1:53). These things are drastic differences from what our world values. Instead, God's justice is magnified for His people. He has a plan and a purpose for His people!

// CAN YOU RELATE TO MARY'S THOUGHT PROCESS IN HER SONG? HOW ARE YOU ENCOURAGED TODAY, KNOWING THAT MARY TRUSTED GOD COMPLETELY DESPITE FEELING UNWORTHY?

This is the place I used to get stuck. I would doubt God and push aside what He was asking me to do because I didn't feel worthy of it. Let alone remotely capable. So I would miss out on every single blessing that comes from following His direction, not to mention the messes I would get myself into because I didn't trust in Him.

Now I don't linger there. Instead, I'm learning to look back and remember how God has shown up in big ways. Fear then subsides a little (not entirely, but a little), and I'm able to work on the thing God has asked me to do. I am now confident that God has my back, and He has yours too.

He has made us worthy for His use. We have a purpose and God has it all planned out.

// TAKE A MOMENT AND WRITE YOUR OWN SONG MAGNIFYING WHAT GOD HAS DONE IN YOUR LIFE. YOU CAN USE MARY'S AS A MODEL OR GET CREATIVE USING WHATEVER STRUCTURE FEELS THE MOST LIKE YOU. EITHER WAY, TAKE SOME TIME TO PRAISE GOD FOR WHAT HE IS DOING IN YOU, THANKING HIM FOR WHAT HE HAS DONE IN THE PAST.

DOER OF THE WORD

How can you apply what you have learned from the Lord today?

_____

_____

_____

_____

SOCIAL CHALLENGE

// **WHAT IS SOMETHING YOU CAN SHARE ABOUT TODAY?**

// **STOP AND ASK GOD TO SHOW YOU WHO TO SHARE THIS WITH TODAY.**

// **WHO SHOULD YOU SHARE THIS WITH? (FINISH SENTENCE BELOW.)**

THIS MESSAGE IS _FOR ALL_ BUT IT IS ALSO FOR:

// **PRAY OVER THAT PERSON(S) OR GROUP AND ASK GOD FOR AN OPPORTUNITY AND COURAGE TO SHARE.**

IF YOU SHARE ON SOCIAL MEDIA
BE SURE TO USE #SACREDHOLIDAYS + TAG @SACREDHOLIDAYS.

BETHLEHEM

By Kat Armstrong

TALK TO GOD

PRAISE // **REPENT** // **ASK** // **YIELD** // **STOP & LISTEN**

My grandmother passed away last year at the age of 94. She was still living independently in the same tiny house she had lived in for 53 years in Harlingen, Texas—and was as tough as nails. Her house was the setting for long, hot, joy-filled summers when I was little. Often, the smell of homemade tortillas woke me up as a child. Her little tiny excuse for a kitchen was where she showed her love through her handmade food. No wonder I love carbs so much.

Later in life that house was the setting for great sadness as my grandmother's lot in life became clearer to me. When she was a young woman, she was a struggling single mother with two kids. She had a middle school education and worked several jobs, including housekeeping and working in a cannery to make ends meet. She was abandoned by two different men over the course of her life, one while she was pregnant. She often wondered how she would put food on the table. My grandmother knew the meaning of hard work in a way I never will; she knew survival.

My mom reminded me last year after my grandmother's funeral that they shared an outhouse with another family and had one light bulb in the house until my mom was in high school. My grandmother fought against the cycle of poverty and conquered it. She was so brave.

I gave her home one last look around as the remaining guests left the funeral reception, and I pondered the way her home marked a place in history that will never be forgotten.

Dr. Luke's eyewitness account of Jesus's life reminded me that every setting has a history and deeply impacts our understanding of everything that happens in that place—just like my grandmother's house.

// READ LUKE 2:1-5 AND NOTE WHO COMMANDED THEY GO AND WHY.

// WHAT DOES THIS SHOW YOU ABOUT THE CHARACTER OF GOD IN YOUR LIFE IN RELATION TO THE AUTHORITIES IN YOUR LIFE, WHETHER THEY BE YOUR GOVERNING OFFICIALS, YOUR BOSS, YOUR TEACHERS, OR YOUR PARENTS?

// READ MICAH 5:2. WHERE DID IT PROPHECY "THE ONE" WHO CAME FOR ALL WOULD COME FROM?

Take for instance, Bethlehem, the setting of Jesus's birth. The word Bethlehem means house of bread. I'm thinking I totally get these carb loving historians. And when I say I love bread, I mean I traced that word though the Bible over the course of a year and wrote a Bible study on it, titled, "I.love.carbs." So I can tell you with authority that bread was always a reminder to His people that He would provide what we need through His presence. Don't miss the fact that the ultimate provision you and I will need in this life is God's presence. He broke through our mess with Jesus's birth in Bethlehem. Jesus is our bread and Bethlehem the bakery.

But Bethlehem had a history that Mary and Joseph would have been familiar with. Their 85-mile journey to Bethlehem to complete the census would have exposed all their vulnerabilities. This young unmarried pregnant couple, bowing to the empire that never should have been in power in the first place, were risking survival.

Jacob lost Rachel on the way to Bethlehem. She was pregnant with Benjamin and died during childbirth. I wonder if Mary and Joseph thought about Rachel on their way to Bethlehem and asked themselves if this trip would also be the death of Mary. Or maybe they stayed the course because they remembered the prophet Micah's words, that although this town is small, it would prove mighty as the birthplace of the Messiah.

In many ways, Sacred Holidays' resources create opportunities to set our own pilgrimage back to these sacred settings. We, too, are on a journey back into our sacred Scriptures to find our Messiah. And so I have to wonder if these familiar places in the Scriptures are exposing the vulnerabilities you feel on your spiritual journey today.

No matter where you are in life's joys and struggles, you and I have hope. Jesus broke through the mess in Bethlehem and promises to stick with us on every journey in life.

// TAKE A MOMENT AND EXPRESS TO GOD THE FEARS YOU FACE IN YOUR JOURNEY.

// NOW LIST OUT THE THINGS THAT COMFORT YOU OR BRING YOU HOPE.

I'm praying a blessing over every reader of this study, that you trade in any short-lived "helps" for the eternal hope of Jesus's presence in your life. If you feel small, weak, vulnerable, or scared, our God is with you and for you, and His presence will be our hope if we would make space for Him in our mess.

DOER OF THE WORD

How can you apply what you have learned from the Lord today?

_____

_____

_____

_____

SOCIAL CHALLENGE

// **WHAT IS SOMETHING YOU CAN SHARE ABOUT TODAY?**

// **STOP AND ASK GOD TO SHOW YOU WHO TO SHARE THIS WITH TODAY.**

// **WHO SHOULD YOU SHARE THIS WITH? (FINISH SENTENCE BELOW.)**

THIS MESSAGE IS *FOR ALL* BUT IT IS ALSO FOR:

// **PRAY OVER THAT PERSON(S) OR GROUP AND ASK GOD FOR AN OPPORTUNITY AND COURAGE TO SHARE.**

IF YOU SHARE ON SOCIAL MEDIA
BE SURE TO USE #SACREDHOLIDAYS + TAG @SACREDHOLIDAYS.

NO ROOM AND THE MANGER

By Lindsay Benedetto

TALK TO GOD

PRAISE // **REPENT** // **ASK** // **YIELD** // **STOP & LISTEN**

I remember feeling like I used to have a full schedule before I had kids. There never seemed to be enough time to do everything. Then I had two babies in less than two years and found out I was pregnant with twins six months after my second was born (insert: all the laughing emojis). I can't even remember what it feels like to sleep all night, let alone have "enough time" to do anything I'd actually like to do. Most days I've reached the end of myself by 9:00 in the morning and my to-do list is ever growing. At least my little humans are still alive, right? In my home, we celebrate the small wins.

The holiday season amplifies my already jam-packed life. January arrives and I hardly know what happened and how I got there. October to December is a complete blur and Christmas is just another day, come and gone. I've missed it; I've missed it so many times. There just simply isn't any room.

// **CAN YOU RELATE? HOW SO?**

I'm often puzzled by this idea that there wasn't room for Mary and Joseph in the inn when they arrived in Bethlehem. My initial thoughts are usually: *How did God let this happen? He knew Mary would be traveling late in her pregnancy. Couldn't He have ensured a comfortable place for her to give birth? Of all the places for Jesus to be laid, why a manger? Ew. We're talking about the Savior of the World, people. This isn't your average baby. How could this happen?*

I know, I know. I can be a bit dramatic. But it's interesting, isn't it? Jesus, the Messiah, the Savior of the world was born in an area where animals were kept, and He was laid in a feeding trough. There simply wasn't any room; it doesn't seem right, does it?

// **WRITE OUT LUKE 2:6-7.**

// **WHY DO YOU THINK GOD ALLOWED THERE TO BE NO ROOM FOR JESUS? WHAT DOES THAT TELL YOU ABOUT HIM?**

Luke's casual and succinct statement is what bothers me initially about this passage. I'm ready to dig in my heels and demand more information! *What do you mean there was no room?! How does this happen?* And then, seemingly unaware of the theological bomb he just dropped, he goes on to talk about the angels appearing to the shepherds. We're expected to leave our questions behind and follow along with his narrative.

A quick Google search will show you there's a lot of controversy surrounding where Jesus was actually born. Some scholars say He was born in a barn or stable; others suggest He was born in the back room of a relative's home. Either way, the undeniable truth in the Christmas story is that there wasn't any room for Mary and Joseph when they arrived in Bethlehem. Whatever accommodations they were given was all that was left. Luke's answer is like any ordinary cause-and-effect answer because there simply just wasn't any room.

I've had this pain in my heart the last several weeks as I've reflected on the idea that there wasn't room for Jesus, because my life is too often like the town of Bethlehem— completely full, no available room.

// **WHAT ABOUT YOU, DO YOU MAKE ROOM FOR JESUS IN YOUR HEART AND LIFE?**

Why is the Christmas season difficult for us to find a few quiet moments to draw near to the One who came near to us? I'm not sure what your story is, but mine usually looks like someone trying extra-hard to accommodate family and friends and work parties, decorating and shopping and church brunches, not to mention traveling and so many other things. Maybe this sounds like you.

It's too much, isn't it? While we fill our time with good things, we let the best thing get away from us. Our lack of room for Jesus is a simple cause-and-effect issue. Our causes might be different, but the effect is always the same: no room.

So how do we combat the busyness of the season and make room for Jesus? I can't answer this question for you; only you can do that. But I think making ourselves available, making room, starts with expectancy. When we make room for Jesus, we can expect that He'll show up in a new way.

I want to leave you with what I consider to be the most beautiful and meaningful part of this passage. As I mentioned, I was irritated by Luke's casual approach to explaining Jesus's birth accommodations (or lack thereof). But as I kept reading, I discovered something I hadn't noticed before.

READ LUKE 2:8-12.

Did you catch it? Verse 12 says, "And this will be a sign for you: you will find a baby wrapped in swaddling cloths and lying in a manger." What's Luke talking about? I think, by and large, he's talking about the fact that there wasn't any room for Jesus. The shepherds could expect to find a baby wrapped in cloths and lying in a manger, because there was no room anywhere else. From the very start, Jesus identifies with the marginalized, the average, and the outcast, foregoing all celestial privilege, taking the form of a man, a baby, and entering our world in less-than-comfortable conditions. In true God-fashion, He uses a political inconvenience to communicate something unique about Himself. He wasn't going to show up as the triumphant King they'd all expected. He'd do the opposite, in fact. He'd make Himself relatable, approachable, common. What beauty and humility!

So many missed it on that Holy night. I don't want to miss it this season. I want to make room for Jesus.

If we take ourselves to the very beginning of this story, we see an absolutely beautiful example of someone who made themselves available for Jesus.

READ LUKE 1:26-38 AND NOTE HOW MARY MADE ROOM FOR JESUS.

If I could be like anyone this Advent season, it would be Mary. This chick straight-up surrenders her life, plans, goals, and dreams in an instant to serve her God. She made herself available without a moment's notice. I'm blown away by this. Can you imagine how scared and confused she must've felt?! Yet she offers the most beautiful response in verse 38, "Behold, I am the servant of the Lord; let it be to me according to your word."

Let's be like Mary this season, ready without a moment's notice to make room, to make ourselves available to Jesus.

As we end our time together, I'd like to do something a little unique. I'd like you to take out your phone or computer, then pull up the song "Oh Light" by Gungor. Let it play over you. Let it encourage you. May you be compelled to make room for the Light who has come. May you be moved to make yourself available to Jesus this Advent season.

AS YOU LISTEN TO THE SONG, ASK GOD TO SHOW YOU HOW TO MAKE ROOM FOR HIM. THEN NOTE SOME NEXT STEPS YOU CAN TAKE TO DO THAT. BE BRAVE AND BOLD HERE! YOU MIGHT WANT TO SEND A PIC OF YOUR NOTES TO SOMEONE WHO WOULD HOLD YOU ACCOUNTABLE TO MAKE ROOM.

DOER OF THE WORD

How can you apply what you have learned from the Lord today?

_____

_____

_____

_____

SOCIAL CHALLENGE

// **WHAT IS SOMETHING YOU CAN SHARE ABOUT TODAY?**

// **STOP AND ASK GOD TO SHOW YOU WHO TO SHARE THIS WITH TODAY.**

// **WHO SHOULD YOU SHARE THIS WITH? (FINISH SENTENCE BELOW.)**

THIS MESSAGE IS *FOR ALL* BUT IT IS ALSO FOR:

// **PRAY OVER THAT PERSON(S) OR GROUP AND ASK GOD FOR AN OPPORTUNITY AND COURAGE TO SHARE.**

IF YOU SHARE ON SOCIAL MEDIA
BE SURE TO USE #SACREDHOLIDAYS + TAG @SACREDHOLIDAYS.

JESUS

By Sharifa Stevens

TALK TO GOD

PRAISE // **REPENT** // **ASK** // **YIELD** // **STOP & LISTEN**

Fully man. Fully God. Messiah. The Good Shepherd. Light of the World. The One we've been waiting for. Every Advent season, we commemorate the hush created when hope and anticipation mingle with the weariness of this broken life. We remember the silence since the last utterances of the prophet Malachi: "'Look! I am sending my messenger, and he will prepare the way before me. Then the Lord you are seeking will suddenly come to his Temple. The messenger of the covenant, whom you look for so eagerly, is surely coming,' says the Lord of Heaven's Armies . . ." (Malachi 3:1).

"Look," the prophet said. And the people of Israel sought that messenger for *four hundred years*. And as the religious experts squinted and scribbled their theories about the Messiah, a virgin conceived and the Christ was born, Isaiah 7:14 was fulfilled, and the center of all time, history, and creation was wrapped in swaddling clothes and placed in a manger.

Jesus fulfilled the prophecies—just not in the way the experts expected, as we will see later on in this session. We'll also explore why Jesus came for us in the first place and why He made the weary world rejoice!

But first let's talk about an important term: *hypostatic union.* Hypostatic union refers to the fact that Jesus has two distinct natures—human and divine—existing in one Person. He is fully man and fully God.

Colossians 2:9 says, "For in Him all the fullness of Deity dwells in bodily form." In other words, Jesus is fully God—the second person of the Trinity who exists eternally and through whom all things originate—but also fully *human,* having been born, tempted, hungry, angry, and ultimately put to death.

Jesus is the Son of Man—the flawless representative of humanity. He knows us because He became one of us in order to save us.

// **READ 1 CORINTHIANS 15:21–22. SUMMARIZE WHAT THESE VERSES SAY ABOUT JESUS.**

Jesus is the triumphant answer to sin and death; His life and death atone the sins **FOR ALL** who believe in Him, and His resurrection is a promise of eternal life **FOR ALL** who put their trust in Him. Where Adam brought death, Jesus brings life.

We have a powerful, compassionate advocate in Jesus.

// **WRITE THE DEFINITION FOR "ADVOCATE" BELOW (ANY REGULAR ENGLISH DICTIONARY WILL WORK).**

// **HOW HAS JESUS BEEN AN ADVOCATE FOR YOU?**

During the 400 years of silence, religious experts continued to look for the Messiah by combing through Scripture, where they discovered many prophecies pointing to the promised One. They knew the Messiah would be the suffering servant (Isaiah 53) of the tribe of Judah (Genesis 49:10), but would also bring prosperity (Amos 9:13) and peace (Isaiah 32:1–8). Choosing to focus more on the latter—on the prophecies pointing to His triumphant victories and less to His crucifixion— the Jewish leaders overlooked a major attribute of Messiah: His ministry to the suffering.

// **TAKING A CLOSER LOOK AT WHY JESUS THE MESSIAH CAME FOR ALL, READ LUKE 4:16–22. WHAT MESSAGE WAS JESUS SENDING TO THOSE LISTENING IN THE SYNAGOGUE? WHAT IS HE ESSENTIALLY SAYING ABOUT HIMSELF IN VERSE 21?**

Jesus didn't just go around from synagogue to synagogue proclaiming, "I am the Messiah!" (Wouldn't that have made things simpler?) Jesus didn't come to gain political power or favor from religious or ruling elites. He came to be the Savior of sinners (Mark 2:17). He made Himself accessible to Samaritans, to women, to lepers, to children, to the blind. He was born of Mary, who was probably slandered her whole life for having a child out of wedlock. Jesus was crucified with sinners, though He was innocent. He is a Savior for the invisible, marginalized, overlooked.

// NOW READ JOHN 1:1-3 AND WRITE OUT WHAT YOU LEARN ABOUT GOD AND HIS SON, JESUS.

These three verses are densely packed with theology, asserting that Jesus is eternal. He was present at the beginning of time, and because He is timeless, He's without beginning or end. Jesus was not only present with God, but He is God. Jesus is the active Creator—the catalyst, the artist, the first cause of creation. He made it all (Colossians 1:16–17).

John 1:14 states that the Word "became flesh" and dwelled with us. He became Emmanuel— "God with us"—so that through Him, we could read God's heart, not from His prophets but directly from His Son, the Word.

In Genesis, God walked in the garden in the cool of the day (Genesis 2:8). He talked to Moses face-to-face, like friends do (Exodus 33:11). Jesus expressed how earnestly He desired to spend Passover with the disciples just hours before His crucifixion (Luke 22:14–15). The physical presence of God was visible during the tabernacle days (Exodus 40:34–38). God, appearing as a pillar of cloud or fire, led the Israelites into rest (Joshua 22:4).

// READ JOHN 8:12. DOES JESUS DECLARE HIMSELF THE LIGHT OF ISRAEL, OR THE LIGHT OF THE WORLD? WHAT ARE THE IMPLICATIONS OF THIS?

Jesus's birth and emptying of Himself to become a man (Philippians 2:6–8) was the ultimate representation of the fact that God is with us—and He wants to be. So much so, that Jesus's presence doesn't end with His ascension in Acts 1. He said, "I go to prepare a place for you. If I go and prepare a place for you, I will come again and receive you to Myself, that where I am, there you may be also" (John 14:2–3).

While we commemorate the Advent of Christ's birth, we still linger in the silence between Jesus's first appearance and the everlasting consummation of His coming kingdom. We wait for that hush of anticipation to be replaced with the awestruck silence of being in Jesus's presence, free from sin, death, and sadness. And unlike the religious experts who missed Jesus even as they looked for Messiah, there will come a day every eye will see Him (Revelation 1:7).

God has always desired to be present in the lives of His people—including our lives . . . right now. The love of Jesus is a relentless pursuit to make God's kingdom a dwelling place with His people, forever.

DOER OF THE WORD

How can you apply what you have learned from the Lord today?

SOCIAL CHALLENGE

// WHAT IS SOMETHING YOU CAN SHARE ABOUT TODAY?

// STOP AND ASK GOD TO SHOW YOU WHO TO SHARE THIS WITH TODAY.

// WHO SHOULD YOU SHARE THIS WITH? (FINISH SENTENCE BELOW.)

THIS MESSAGE IS *FOR ALL* BUT IT IS ALSO FOR:

// PRAY OVER THAT PERSON(S) OR GROUP AND ASK GOD FOR AN OPPORTUNITY AND COURAGE TO SHARE.

IF YOU SHARE ON SOCIAL MEDIA
BE SURE TO USE #SACREDHOLIDAYS + TAG @SACREDHOLIDAYS.

SHEPHERDS

By Rachel Joy

TALK TO GOD

PRAISE // **REPENT** // **ASK** // **YIELD** // **STOP & LISTEN**

A pendulum swing exists in our society today between pride and pride. Yes, you read that correctly; it's not a typo! Pride and pride have become the norm in relating to the world and people around us. The center of the pendulum is where we find true, deeply rooted in Christ, abiding humility. But the pendulum often swings to one side, where we find an arrogant pride that boasts of one's accomplishments, beauty, intellect, giftings, etc. However, on the other side of the pendulum exists an equally dangerous, internal pride that masks itself as humility. Self-deprecation and/or self-reliance rule below the surface of such pride. Either way, there's a self-focus that can build a sense of superiority.

We live in a culture that has coined the phrase, "humble brag." This should clue us into our society's climate of pride. With the rise of social media as a major avenue for communication and community, we have seen an increase in both self-promotion and self-deprecation. Pride does not discriminate; it runs rampant among believers and non-believers alike. The enemy uses pride to fog our vision with "self" and distract us from our purpose as followers of Christ. However, true humility is found in the person and the work of Jesus Christ.

// **READ PHILIPPIANS 2:5-11 AND MAKE NOTE OF THE WAYS IN WHICH JESUS EMBODIED HUMILITY.**

//   NOW READ PHILIPPIANS 2:3-4. IN LIGHT OF WHO JESUS IS AND HIS PERFECT EXAMPLE OF HUMILITY, WHAT IS PAUL'S ENCOURAGEMENT TO US AS BELIEVERS?

Imagine taking on this perspective, viewing each action in your day-to-day life as an opportunity to exercise true humility. True peace is found when we make much of Christ and count others better than ourselves. Then we are able to freely serve and experience joy!

//   HOW CAN YOU PRACTICALLY MODEL CHRIST'S HUMILITY IN YOUR DAY-TO-DAY LIFE?

Each Advent season, as I read the Christmas story, the attribute of humility continues to leap off the pages to me. The God of the universe put on flesh and came into this world in the most humble way possible, as a baby. By humility, Jesus would restore our humanity. He could have come in a variety of majestic ways, but He chose a humble state. Furthermore, what is truly mind-boggling is God chose a group of humble men to be the first to hear of the Messiah's birth.

//   READ LUKE 2:8-18. WHO DID GOD CHOOSE TO TELL FIRST ABOUT THE BIRTH OF JESUS?

Shepherds at one time were held in high esteem among God's people. However, at the time of our Savior's birth, they held a lowly position in society. They were unbecoming, unwanted, and unimportant. That's a lot of "uns!" Living on the outskirts of town, they tended to sheep and were considered dirty outcasts. Yet, God chose to reveal the arrival of the King of Kings to shepherds first.

//   IN YOUR OWN OPINION, WHY DO YOU THINK HE CHOSE THIS GROUP OF MEN?

Jesus is the perfect example of humility, but throughout Scripture we see other humble men and women we can learn from, and the shepherds are no different! Don't let these lowly men fool you; they are worth our attention and study, and so much can be gleaned from their way of life!

//   READING LUKE 2:8-18 ONCE MORE, JOT DOWN THE WAYS IN WHICH THE SHEPHERDS WERE HUMBLE.

Humility involves both the posture of your heart and the actions that flow from that posture.

The shepherds showed us four postures and actions in Luke 2 that we, as Christ followers, should strive for in our own lives. First, shepherds serve. No matter the task at hand, shepherds served and laid down their own safety for the flock in their care. Second, shepherds watch. The shepherd's job was to be watchful not only of the sheep, but for whatever they would experience in the wilderness. With their eyes open, they remained expectant and attune to the world around them, not becoming comfortable in their surroundings or their own abilities. Third, shepherds receive. The shepherds, upon hearing the good news of the Messiah, humbly received it. Finally, shepherds move. The shepherds immediately moved with the news to Bethlehem, anxious to see the Savior of the world, and then proclaimed what they had heard from the angel!

Throughout Scripture God identifies Himself as a Shepherd, as one who serves, watches, receives, and moves.

// IN THE FOLLOWING PASSAGES, HOW DOES GOD CARE FOR AND LOVE HIS PEOPLE AS A SHEPHERD?

PSALM 23:1-6

ISAIAH 40:11

EZEKIEL 34:11-16

We must not miss the importance of why God chose to reveal the birth of the Savior of the world to shepherds! The news was revealed to shepherds to reflect God's heart and God's plan for His children.

Jesus's birth is announced to shepherds to remind us of the depth of the Shepherd's consistent care and love for us—that He would send the Good Shepherd (John 10:1-18) to live a sinless life, take on the sin's of the world, and lay down His life for you, me, and the rest of the world.

// READ AND WRITE OUT LUKE 2:10. THEN UNDERLINE THE WORDS "FOR ALL."

The coming of the long-awaited Messiah is **For All** people. Jesus came to ransom and reconcile all those who God has called according to His purpose. This means, no matter where you are, what you've done, the shame you carry, or how unlovable you feel—you cannot escape God's love. God loves you right where you are and He has provided a way for all people to be in a relationship with Him through His Son, Jesus. As we hear this good news once more this Advent season, or maybe receive it for the first time, let's not forget to humbly watch for every opportunity to share it with the world around us!

DOER OF THE WORD

How can you apply what you have learned from the Lord today?

SOCIAL CHALLENGE

// **WHAT IS SOMETHING YOU CAN SHARE ABOUT TODAY?**

// **STOP AND ASK GOD TO SHOW YOU WHO TO SHARE THIS WITH TODAY.**

// **WHO SHOULD YOU SHARE THIS WITH? (FINISH SENTENCE BELOW.)**

THIS MESSAGE IS *FOR ALL* BUT IT IS ALSO FOR:

// **PRAY OVER THAT PERSON(S) OR GROUP AND ASK GOD FOR AN OPPORTUNITY AND COURAGE TO SHARE.**

IF YOU SHARE ON SOCIAL MEDIA
BE SURE TO USE #SACREDHOLIDAYS + TAG @SACREDHOLIDAYS.

ANGELS

By Heather Brock

TALK TO GOD

PRAISE // REPENT // ASK // YIELD // STOP & LISTEN

I closed the foster care book I had been reading, mulling over the difficult situations that filled its pages. I had been longing to adopt a child for as long as I could remember, and no amount of warning of difficulty would take that away, but I could still feel the fear rising in my throat. I had faced the same fear with my third baby slowly growing inside me. What if this child will be too difficult for me to handle? What if this breaks me? What if I won't be enough as a mother?

Zacharias, Elizabeth, Mary, and Joseph were expecting babies, too, and the fears they must have faced could have dwarfed mine ten-fold. It started when the angel Gabriel showed up in the temple with Zacharias. Fear gripped him.

// READ LUKE 1:13. WHAT WAS GABRIEL'S FIRST MESSAGE TO HIM, BEFORE HE ANNOUNCED ANYTHING ELSE?

The next person Gabriel visited with a similar message was Mary. She didn't seem as afraid of the angel himself, but she was perplexed by being called "favored one" and by his statement that the Lord was with her. *What kind of a greeting is that?* she thought.

// READ LUKE 1:30. WHAT WAS THE ANGEL'S FIRST MESSAGE TO HER?

In a dream, another angel (perhaps Gabriel—we are not told) visited Joseph. Again, we're not told that he is scared by the angel, but we can guess at the state of Joseph's heart towards the news that his betrothed, Mary, was pregnant, when we hear the angel's first words to him:

// READ MATTHEW 1:20. WHAT WERE THE ANGEL'S FIRST WORDS TO JOSEPH?

Even after Jesus was born, the angel visiting the shepherds, blinding them in the middle of the black night with the glory of the Lord and terrifying the wits out of them, had the same message: "Do not be afraid" (Luke 2:9).

Think about it. The advent story is rife with opportunities for abject fear—angels appearing, voices taken away, miraculous pregnancies, a seemingly unfaithful fiancée, probable rejection from an entire community, possible death by stoning, labor pains coming fast amid the fruitless search for an appropriate birthing room in a new city, a jealous king seeking the life of the baby, and much long travel through difficult terrain where marauders could be lurking behind any large rock.

These people had a right to fear, didn't they? However, what did God say through His messengers to almost every one of the players in this story?

// NOW WRITE DOWN WHAT GOD SAID THROUGH HIS MESSENGERS—IN UPPER CASE LETTERS!

How do we not stay drowning in fear, especially when we are facing real difficulties like Mary and Joseph faced? How do we even stay clear of anxious, stressed-out thoughts around the busyness of Christmastime? After all, sometimes the small responsibilities add up to large challenges.

I don't know how the people in the advent story handled their fear. Hopefully they heeded the words of the angels. Thankfully, God has given us a beautiful prescription For All in Philippians 4:6-8: "Be anxious for nothing, but in everything by prayer and supplication with thanksgiving let your requests be made known to God. And the peace of God, which surpasses all comprehension, will guard your hearts and your minds in Christ Jesus. Finally, brethren, whatever is true, whatever is honorable, whatever is right, whatever is pure, whatever is lovely, whatever is of good repute, if there is any excellence and if anything worthy of praise, dwell on these things."

First, ask God for help. ". . . let your requests be made known to God."

God, if the child we take into our home to foster is struggling mightily due to the trauma received, please give us the ability to love him well.

Lord, please help me finish all the Christmas tasks that need to be completed in the time I have.

Help me know which I really do need to complete and which I can drop.

Father, please heal my mother from her accident.

Second, thank God, putting your trust in Him while doing so. ". . . with thanksgiving . . ."

Thank You, God, that you can easily give me the strength to take care of my baby when she's born, no matter her temperament.

Thank You, Heavenly Father, that you have always been there for me in the past and will always be there for me in the future.

Father, thank you for knowing what I need more than I do, for caring about my needs, and for being powerful enough to take care of me.

Third, focus on the good. ". . . whatever is true, whatever is honorable, whatever is right, whatever is pure, whatever is lovely, whatever is of good repute, if there is any excellence and if anything worthy of praise, dwell on these things."

I have a lot to do for my family around Christmastime, but I'm glad I have family with which to spend it.

Yes, my son is sick, but look at how well he's bearing up under it! I can see how God is using it to build his perseverance.

I don't know if I'll make it to the airport on time, but I'm thankful we had the money this year to travel at all.

> **AS YOU DWELL ON THE LAST POINT—FOCUS ON THE GOOD—WRITE DOWN THREE GOOD THINGS YOU SEE HAPPENING ALL AROUND YOU.**

As I have considered the trials that may lie ahead through fostering a troubled child, stretching me to the limit, I've decided to bring every fear I have to the Father, trusting my worthy God with thanksgiving for the help He will give me. I have chosen to focus on all the ways He has never failed me in the past. He didn't fail Zacharias, Mary, Joseph, Elizabeth, or the shepherds. I know He will never fail me, either, no matter my fears.

DOER OF THE WORD

How can you apply what you have learned from the Lord today?

_____

_____

_____

_____

SOCIAL CHALLENGE

// **WHAT IS SOMETHING YOU CAN SHARE ABOUT TODAY?**

// **STOP AND ASK GOD TO SHOW YOU WHO TO SHARE THIS WITH TODAY.**

// **WHO SHOULD YOU SHARE THIS WITH? (FINISH SENTENCE BELOW.)**

THIS MESSAGE IS _FOR ALL_ BUT IT IS ALSO FOR:

// **PRAY OVER THAT PERSON(S) OR GROUP AND ASK GOD FOR AN OPPORTUNITY AND COURAGE TO SHARE.**

IF YOU SHARE ON SOCIAL MEDIA
BE SURE TO USE #SACREDHOLIDAYS + TAG @SACREDHOLIDAYS.

WISE MEN

By Kelly King

TALK TO GOD

PRAISE // REPENT // ASK // YIELD // STOP & LISTEN

My son was five-years-old when he was chosen to portray the young Jesus accepting the gifts of gold, frankincense, and myrrh from the wise men in our church's annual Christmas production. My fair-skinned, blue-eyed, red-headed little boy had no resemblance of the Christ-child, but this didn't distract him from taking the role very seriously. Each night of the performance, he would stand stoically next to Mary and Joseph as the wise men made their grand entrance complete with pomp and circumstance. There were no lines to memorize and no choreographed movements. His only job was to stand still (that's hard enough for little boys) and watch the wise men bow and lay gifts at his feet.

Though more than 20 years ago, that particular memory has caused me many times to consider the role of the wise men in the Christmas story. I've often wondered about the timing of their arrival, their long journey, and how their encounter with Immanuel—God with us—changed their lives.

// **DESCRIBE A LIFE-CHANGING MOMENT, A TIME YOU EXPERIENCE GOD WITH YOU.**

The story of the magi from the east is found in Matthew chapter 2 and their story is often incorrectly told. Traditional Christmas accounts tend to place them at the manger on the night Christ was born, yet it was more likely their arrival didn't happen for several months, even up to two years. We traditionally say there were three of them, yet Scripture never indicates their exact number. We tend to base this off of the three gifts. But who were these guys?

First, we know the wise men came from the East during the time of King Herod. Magi were often scholars and astrologers. They were not Jews, a reminder that Jesus's arrival was for everyone—not just Israel. Many people during this time in history were fascinated by historical events that correlated to galactic occurrences. The original language for magi is compared to Babylonian priests or men gifted in dream interpretation, much like those found in the book of Daniel. They had read the prophecies and were aware that Jews eagerly anticipated a King— even though it had been hundreds of years since the original prophecy in Micah. These wise men were not just led by a star, but by the revelation of God's Word. It's a reminder for all of us to be led first by Scripture and not the opinions of men or creation.

// **WHEN ARE YOU TEMPTED TO BE LED BY THE OPINIONS OF THOSE AROUND YOU INSTEAD OF GOD'S WORD?**

Making their way to Bethlehem, they first stopped and paid King Herod a visit. Leaving King Herod, the Wise Men made their way to the house where Jesus was. Scripture says in Matthew 2:9-10, "After hearing the king, they went on their way. And there it was—the star they had seen at its rising. It led them until it came and stopped above the place where the child was. When they saw the star, they were overwhelmed with joy."

As an act of worship, they bowed before the child and delivered gifts of gold, frankincense, and myrrh. Not only were these extravagant gifts, they were symbolic and significant. The gold represented Jesus's position as King, the incense was symbolic of Jesus as our High Priest, and the myrrh was symbolic of His death, a foreshadowing of what would happen on the cross.

// **WHAT IS ONE VISIBLE AND TANGIBLE ACT OF WORSHIP YOU CAN GIVE TO YOUR SAVIOR THIS WEEK?**

Following their visit, both the wise men and Joseph received warnings in the form of dreams. We never hear of the wise men again, yet we know they returned home without paying Herod a return visit. Surely they returned, telling the story again and again for the rest of their lives— they met Jesus. We never hear of the star again, yet we know Joseph fled Bethlehem and the family settled in Egypt until Herod's death. Surely the gold given by the wise men became a practical gift to sustain them during this time.

You and I can learn so much from the few verses of Scripture surrounding the wise men's visit to young Jesus. We learn God reveals Himself in a multitude of ways and **For All** people—from the lowliest of shepherds to the scholarly magi. We are reminded that when we truly worship, we are humbled, whether we physically fall to our knees in adoration or bend our hearts toward Him. Like the wise men, let's spend more effort focused on what we will give Christ rather than on the gifts under our trees. He's ready to use what you bring: your finances, your time, and your talents. Most of all, when we truly encounter Jesus, our lives are forever changed, compelling us to share our story for the rest of our earthly lives.

DOER OF THE WORD

How can you apply what you have learned from the Lord today?

_____

_____

_____

_____

SOCIAL CHALLENGE

// **WHAT IS SOMETHING YOU CAN SHARE ABOUT TODAY?**

// **STOP AND ASK GOD TO SHOW YOU WHO TO SHARE THIS WITH TODAY.**

// **WHO SHOULD YOU SHARE THIS WITH? (FINISH SENTENCE BELOW.)**

THIS MESSAGE IS _FOR ALL_ BUT IT IS ALSO FOR:

// **PRAY OVER THAT PERSON(S) OR GROUP AND ASK GOD FOR AN OPPORTUNITY AND COURAGE TO SHARE.**

IF YOU SHARE ON SOCIAL MEDIA
BE SURE TO USE #SACREDHOLIDAYS + TAG @SACREDHOLIDAYS.

KING HEROD AND SCRIBES

By Molly Parker

TALK TO GOD

PRAISE // REPENT // ASK // YIELD // STOP & LISTEN

Almost two years after the birth of our Savior, a dusty caravan from the East made its grand entrance into Jerusalem. When this caravan of Messiah-seeking astrologers—the wise men—stopped to ask, "Where is He who has been born King of the Jews? For we have seen His star and have come to worship Him" (Matthew 2:2), fear and terror filled the heart of a much lesser king: "Herod the Great." Or, more fittingly, Herod the not-so Great.

// READ MATTHEW 2:1-3. LIST THE POSSIBLE REASONS WHY KING HEROD WAS DISTURBED.

For starters, the wise men didn't come looking for Herod; they had no interest in him, which must have been a blow to his ego. I imagine Herod felt the same way we feel—times a million—when we're at a party, and the people we're chatting with keep looking over our shoulders for someone more interesting. After all, according to Herod, who could possibly be more fascinating than him? The man who wormed his way to the top, who was appointed king of Judaea, and who built palaces, fortresses, and lavish cities. A tyrant who had so much power, he killed-off people in his own family, causing Caesar Augustus to suggest, "It is safer to be Herod's pig than his son."

Without a doubt, Herod did whatever it took to exalt himself and secure a spot as front runner for the most interesting man in the world. But on that day, someone far more intriguing and praiseworthy and glorious was being sought.

Looking deeper, beyond the bruised ego, we see the main reason why Herod became upset; we find it in the wise men's question, "Where is He who has been born King of the Jews?" It's a question that sent Herod's mind to spinning: What if they're onto something? What if there really is a true King? What if the nation of Israel rallies around Him and I get the boot?

// **READ MATTHEW 2:4-6. WHY DO YOU THINK THE CHIEF PRIESTS AND SCRIBES WERE ABLE TO RESPOND SO QUICKLY TO HEROD'S INQUIRY OF WHERE THE CHRIST WAS TO BE BORN?**

Turns out the Jewish leaders knew their stuff. Because the scribes meticulously wrote-out and memorized Scripture, referencing Micah 5:2 in verses 5 and 6, it's no wonder "Bethlehem" was on the tip of their tongue. And there couldn't have been a more perfect place for Jesus to be born, for He came into the world through Bethlehem, which means, "House of Bread."

// **WRITE DOWN JOHN 6:35.**

What a beautiful detail hidden in the Christmas story! The Bread of Life was born in the House of Bread. By comparing Himself to bread, Jesus is telling us He is essential to life; only through Him are we nourished, satisfied, filled, and given eternal life. No earthly bread can do that.

// **READ MATTHEW 2:7-11 AND NOTE THE DETAILS OF THE STORY.**

It's obvious Herod was faking interest in worshipping the young Child, or he would have gone with the wise men. But why did the Jewish religious leaders stay back, considering they knew of the prophecies that pointed to Bethlehem as the Messiah's hometown?

// **WRITE DOWN WHY YOU THINK THE RELIGIOUS LEADERS STAYED BACK.**

Because the chief priests and scribes were more interested in possessing a vast knowledge of Scripture, earning the respect of the people, and maintaining an outward appearance of perfection, they were blinded to receiving the promised Messiah. Laboring over food that perishes—the "earthly bread" of knowledge, reputation, and good deeds—they completely missed the one thing God wanted them to seek: Jesus, the One who came *For All.*

I often see myself in the Jewish leaders. Sometimes I'll join Bible studies or attend prayer meetings in an attempt to gain influence or simply because I'm "supposed" to. Instead of allowing God's love to be the motivating force behind all that I do, my own desires and whims take over, leaving me unsatisfied and feeling disconnected from my Savior. Like the religious leaders, I, too, have tasted of the same perishable bread, the same stale crust of hollow routine—and have been found wanting. Thankfully, Jesus is compassionate and gracious, slow to anger, abounding in love, and fills me the moment I put my focus back on Him.

NOW READ MATTHEW 2:12 AND NOTE WHAT THE WISE MEN DID.

Not only were the wise men students of the sky, they also studied dreams. How wonderful that our God met them in a place of personal interest.

HAS GOD EVER GOTTEN YOUR ATTENTION IN A UNIQUE WAY . . . IN A WAY THAT SUITED YOU, THAT HAD YOUR NAME WRITTEN ALL OVER IT?

READ MATTHEW 2:16-18 AND NOTE WHAT HAPPENED.

And here we see yet another side of the Christmas story—a horrific turn of events predicted long ago in Jeremiah 31:15. How arrogant of Herod to think, All I have to do is kill the babe in Bethlehem; that should stop Him from taking my place! As if anything or anyone on earth could stop the "one who will be ruler over Israel, whose origins are from old, from ancient times" (Micah 5:2b). Jesus has always been and always will be.

And because we serve a God who doesn't leave lives in ruin, we know it doesn't end there.

READ AND WRITE OUT JEREMIAH 31:16-17, THEN CIRCLE GOD'S PROMISES.

As we end our study of King Herod's cowardly involvement in the Christmas story, we can be thankful God did not meet His match in Herod. Though people may scheme-up evil, God's plans cannot be thwarted (Job 42:2), and His purposes will always prevail (Proverbs 19:21).

DOER OF THE WORD

How can you apply what you have learned from the Lord today?

SOCIAL CHALLENGE

// **WHAT IS SOMETHING YOU CAN SHARE ABOUT TODAY?**

// **STOP AND ASK GOD TO SHOW YOU WHO TO SHARE THIS WITH TODAY.**

// **WHO SHOULD YOU SHARE THIS WITH? (FINISH SENTENCE BELOW.)**

THIS MESSAGE IS *FOR ALL* BUT IT IS ALSO FOR:

// **PRAY OVER THAT PERSON(S) OR GROUP AND ASK GOD FOR AN OPPORTUNITY AND COURAGE TO SHARE.**

IF YOU SHARE ON SOCIAL MEDIA
BE SURE TO USE #SACREDHOLIDAYS + TAG @SACREDHOLIDAYS.

THE FIRST SEVEN DAYS

By Melanie Dale

TALK TO GOD

PRAISE // REPENT // ASK // YIELD // STOP & LISTEN

Today we are going to take some creative freedom with the Christmas story. There is nothing written in those days between Jesus being born and Him being circumcised. While nothing is mentioned, we can use our imaginations, knowing Mary was a woman who had just had a baby, even if He was the Son of God.

I remember the first time I tried to nurse my four-pound preemie son in the hospital. I was a brand new mom with zero baby experience and my boob was bigger than his head. The nurse handed him to me and helped shove my nipple into his tiny mouth, and I worried she'd break him.

I wish I could picture what Jesus's life was like during his first week on earth, but honestly I can't. First, because it's Jesus and no precedents have been set for saviors being born human. Second, my son spent his first week in the NICU hooked-up to beeping things, so I'm not sure what all goes on in the first week of a new human's life outside of the short visits I was afforded to hold him with sterilized hands.

No, when I try to visualize those first moments after Jesus's birth, I don't actually think about Jesus. Rather, I think about His very human mom. I don't know about babies, but I do know about mothering and perhaps some of what Mary experienced.

// **TODAY IS MORE IMAGINATIVE THAN BIBLE STUDY. WHAT DO YOU IMAGINE THAT FIRST WEEK WAS LIKE FOR THIS LITTLE FAMILY?**

Even as she held Jesus in her arms, her body continued to expel the remains of her pregnancy. The song, "Away in a Manger," has it wrong when it claims, "No crying He makes." If you've ever been present after a delivery, you know good and well there's some crying, and it's a good thing too. Crying means clear, healthy lungs, so we want to hear wailing. That first wail signified to Mary that her work of labor and delivery was over—and her work of parenting was just beginning.

A couple days later her milk came in, and nursing was sweet relief to her engorged breasts. And I wonder if it came easily or if Mary spent those first few days trying to figure out a good latch to help Jesus receive the nutrients He needed. Did she call La Leche League in a panic or send Joseph for the innkeeper's wife to ask if she's doing it right? Did she beg God to please, please, please help Him latch before her nipple wore clean off?

I spent that first week waddling around in those hospital mesh panties and pads as big as twin-sized mattresses. My body felt tender, like it'd been pounded over with a meat mallet, and it hurt when I laughed.

My son wasn't the Messiah, but he was my little miracle, born after a long battle with infertility. My mind hummed with the wonder of him. His tiny existence filled my heart to the brim and I was all love and bodily fluids leaking out of every nook and cranny. The nurses, doctors, and well-wishers kept coming, and I simply wanted to cradle my child in my tired arms—just the two of us.

How strange to think about our Savior needing Mary, His human mother. He lowered Himself, coming down to dwell among us, allowing Himself to "need." Completely helpless in His infant state, He was fully God and also fully reliant on a first-time mother to breastfeed Him, to clean His body, to keep Him safe. What a heady experience for Mary and Joseph.

// WHAT DO YOU THINK OF THIS IDEA, THAT JESUS WAS A HELPLESS BABY? HAVE YOU EVER CONSIDERED THIS ABOUT HIM BEFORE?

I remember the first rush of protectiveness I felt as a mother for my son. A car cut us off on the freeway, and I yelled at the driver, "BABY ON BOARD," with the biggest mama bear growl I could muster. I felt the full weight of responsibility rest on me to make sure this child thrived and grew, with his wobbly neck and soft spot on his skull.

After the rush and activity of delivery, the emotions flooded over me as the days passed. I wonder if Mary paused to let tears stream uninhibited from her eyes. Tears, laughter, all the emotions created by the very God she birthed, streaming out of her in a cathartic gush. I imagine Joseph tended her gently.

There's a reason the Bible cloaks with mystery these interim days post-birth, pre-circumcision. That first week is for visceral healing, for rest, for gaining strength, and for becoming a family.

I think about this week before the world pushed in, before He was circumcised and presented at the temple, when they were a family of three. These precious moments together were for bonding. The cycle of Jesus having a need and Mary meeting that need created healthy neurological pathways in Jesus's brain. Together they developed trust and love.

We read so much about His public ministry on earth, but His time here began in private, alone with loving parents, receiving nourishment and protection. He arrived in the quiet, in a whisper, needing His parents until He "grew in wisdom and stature, and in favor with God and man" (Luke 2:52), completely prepared For All who needed Him.

DOER OF THE WORD

How can you apply what you have learned from the Lord today?

SOCIAL CHALLENGE

// **WHAT IS SOMETHING YOU CAN SHARE ABOUT TODAY?**

// **STOP AND ASK GOD TO SHOW YOU WHO TO SHARE THIS WITH TODAY.**

// **WHO SHOULD YOU SHARE THIS WITH? (FINISH SENTENCE BELOW.)**

THIS MESSAGE IS *FOR ALL* BUT IT IS ALSO FOR:

// **PRAY OVER THAT PERSON(S) OR GROUP AND ASK GOD FOR AN OPPORTUNITY AND COURAGE TO SHARE.**

IF YOU SHARE ON SOCIAL MEDIA
BE SURE TO USE #SACREDHOLIDAYS + TAG @SACREDHOLIDAYS.

SIMEON

By Osheta Moore

TALK TO GOD

PRAISE // REPENT // ASK // YIELD // STOP & LISTEN

_____

_____

_____

_____

Before we moved to Saint Paul, my husband was the associate pastor of a church in Los Angeles for three years. When he was offered the job, we were living in Boston, so we were faced with a question: *Should we move our family across the country to serve at a church that regularly reached the homeless community in downtown Los Angeles?* We did, and our move from Boston to L.A. ushered in a season full of even more questions: *Will we make friendships? Will we be able to balance family and ministry work? What would our daily rhythms look like now that we're no longer dealing with snow five months out the year? What about my calling to be writer?*

It felt like everything was unstable and out of my control. Many nights I cried myself to sleep because the transition to a new city was taking longer than I had hoped. It felt like God didn't see me or know that I was hurting. Even worse, I wondered if God forgot that He promised to never leave or forsake me.

// **HAVE YOU EVER FELT THAT GOD HAS FORGOTTEN YOU? DESCRIBE THE CIRCUMSTANCES.**

In the weeks following our move, I would text my friends back in Boston and ask for prayer (or a virtual hug) because I so wanted to see God in the midst of all the questions and all the instability, but I couldn't. One day, after a teary text conversation with a friend, she picked up the phone and called me to say she was praying for me and she felt the Lord wanted her to tell me,

"Osheta, this season of transition is going to take time and that's okay. Lean into the love of Jesus right now. Be patient. God sees you and he knows your needs." In a nutshell, my friend was encouraging me to wait well.

This is where we find Simeon and the Judeans in our passage today. They have been waiting for years for their Messiah to come. They felt a mixture of sorrow and confusion. Because of the Roman oppression, they wondered if God forgot that He promised His people shalom-flourishing wholeness and peace. Yet there is one man, Simeon, who had been, according to theologian Walter Brueggemann, "waiting in patient hope."

// **READ LUKE 2:25-26. LIST WHAT SCRIPTURE SAYS ABOUT SIMEON.**

Simeon had a living, dynamic relationship with the Lord and because of this, he trusted God—even though everything around him said he couldn't. He waited well with a patient hope that said, "No matter what, I will believe with my whole heart that God sees me and knows my needs."

I want to wait well like this. Maybe you do too.

// **DO YOU REMEMBER A TIME YOU WAITED WITH A PATIENT HOPE? HOW DID GOD REVEAL HIMSELF TO YOU OR ANSWER YOUR PRAYER? ARE YOU STILL WAITING?**

In our world today, we need Jesus followers who are willing to wait well by choosing joy in the waiting, rejecting anxiety, and clinging to hope. In order to do this it would help to have the same kind of picture of God that Simeon had: God is good and keeps His promises. This is why Simeon broke out in praise and knew he could die in peace, all because Jesus showed up! He even said in Luke 2:29, "Sovereign Lord, now let your servant die in peace, as you have promised. I have seen your salvation, which you have prepared for all people."

He held in his very hands the evidence that God sees us, God knows our needs, and God answers prayers. He's trustworthy and full of integrity. His sovereignty is beautiful in that God is who he says He is: our deliverer in hard times and oh so trustworthy.

// **WHEN YOU THINK OF GOD, THE ONE IN WHOM YOU'RE TRUSTING WITH YOUR FEARS AND WORRIES, WHO DO YOU SEE?**

Some see God as a stingy Daddy Warbucks, or secretly think He has the resources to make things happen but on purpose doesn't show up until people are at their lowest and most in need. If that's how you picture God in your waiting, then it's no surprise that joy is hard to find. I've felt this way about God, but thankfully, this is not the picture of God that Jesus portrays.

Once my kids asked me if there was another reason why Jesus came to earth. After all, it didn't make sense for a baby to be born, just to die for the world 33 years later. And I told them yes, there's so much more! Jesus came **For All,** not just to live a holy life and model self-giving love by dying on the cross where He took the punishment for our sins, He came to show us the character of God as a loving father, who genuinely cares about our suffering and desires to be close to us as we wait. Jesus came so that He can hold us with human arms, restore the outcasts, identify with our brokenness, and have firsthand knowledge of our suffering.

As we look at the darkness around us this Advent, let us not forget that there is light at the end—we get to celebrate the birth of Jesus. Let us be women who treasure the promises of God in our hearts. Let us hold on to hope patiently, joyfully, and intentionally. Let our patient hope inspire those around us so they, too, will seek to know Jesus, the Light of the World and Prince of Peace.

DOER OF THE WORD

How can you apply what you have learned from the Lord today?

SOCIAL CHALLENGE

// **WHAT IS SOMETHING YOU CAN SHARE ABOUT TODAY?**

// **STOP AND ASK GOD TO SHOW YOU WHO TO SHARE THIS WITH TODAY.**

// **WHO SHOULD YOU SHARE THIS WITH? (FINISH SENTENCE BELOW.)**

THIS MESSAGE IS *FOR ALL* BUT IT IS ALSO FOR:

// **PRAY OVER THAT PERSON(S) OR GROUP AND ASK GOD FOR AN OPPORTUNITY AND COURAGE TO SHARE.**

IF YOU SHARE ON SOCIAL MEDIA
BE SURE TO USE #SACREDHOLIDAYS + TAG @SACREDHOLIDAYS.

ANNA

By Jen Weaver

TALK TO GOD

PRAISE // REPENT // ASK // YIELD // STOP & LISTEN

Most people associate Christmas time with happiness. Our memories flood with recollections of laughter and festive gatherings. But some of us face the holidays with twinges of sadness as we recall a happy season gone by, the loss of a loved one, or wishes that remain unfulfilled.

My Decembers bring a lot of joy, but also stand as a reminder of two children I carried in my womb but never got to hold in my arms. The first was an early term miscarriage, bleeding that started while attending our church's Christmas production. The second, a surprise pregnancy announcement to my parents on Christmas morning, only to learn a few short weeks later that our baby no longer had a heartbeat.

I'm reminded of these experiences as I read the story of Anna in Luke 2.

// **READ LUKE 2:36–39. WHAT WAS ANNA'S HEARTACHE?**

Now a widow advanced in years, Hannah spent most of her life in the temple. I doubt that's the existence she expected. What new bride anticipates a lifetime commitment only lasting seven years? What wife plans to live most of her years as a widow? Scripture doesn't tell us why Anna began spending her days in the temple, but I wonder if she first arrived in anguish as she mourned the recent loss of her husband and the failed plans for their future together.

While heartbreaking, I appreciate this visual because Anna didn't run from God or try to hide her pain. I believe she knew that the Lord heals burdened hearts and comforts those who weep with bitter tears, so she brought herself to His presence in a time of her greatest sorrow.

// **HOW HAVE YOU RESPONDED TO YOUR MOST RECENT SORROW?**

I, too, learned from my seasons of loss that God can handle my mess. I don't need to stay distant from His Presence while I work through the pain and sadness on my own—He wants me to bring it to Him so He can help me through it. Thus I refuse to withhold my heart from Jesus. As I reflect on what I've lost in the past, or during a present sadness, I bring my heartache to His feet. I let pain prompt me to pray. When my thoughts turn to what could have been, or what never was, I also instruct my heart to worship. It's not always easy to refocus my attention on Jesus, but the more I choose the perspective I want to have, the easier it becomes. First comes my choice to draw near.

// **ARE YOU LETTING ANY HEARTACHE OR DIFFICULTIES KEEP YOU AWAY FROM GOD? HOW CAN YOU TURN THAT INTO MOTIVATION TO COME TO HIM INSTEAD?**

Every time we enter God's presence, we receive healing. The Lord doesn't comfort our hearts so we can stay in the same spot, with a slightly lesser pain. He brings us out of it. I think Anna found this, too, because as the years passed, she never left God's presence. Perhaps she found hope in Psalm 30, a song of David when the temple was first dedicated.

// **READ PSALM 30, AND WRITE OUT VERSES 5, 11–12.**

Anna may have come to the temple with wailing, but over the years God turned her pain into praise. Even if the initial days or weeks carried grief, I think it's safe to assume that eighty years in, she was asking God to answer a different prayer.

She waited for the Savior, and God again turned her mourning into rejoicing because she was one of two people who got to interact with baby Jesus on the day of His consecration.

// **READ LUKE 2:38 AGAIN. WHAT CAUSED ANNA'S REJOICING?**

I love how Anna recognized the Messiah even in baby human form. As soon as He entered—at that very moment—she gave thanks. I believe Anna saw Him so quickly because she watched for Him. Day and night, she worshipped in the temple with prayer and fasting. She listened for word of His coming, and on this celebratory day in Luke chapter 2, she noticed when He arrived.

As believers, we too are looking for Jesus. Thankfully, we don't need to wait for eighty years to see our Messiah, our Savior. He's already here. Yes, this season may carry difficulty and disappointment. But it's also a reminder that our God is with us. Our Savior lives. Just like He did with Anna, God calls us near to Him today, mess and all, to bring healing to our hearts. He wants to turn our mourning into rejoicing.

HOW CAN YOU LOOK FOR JESUS IN THE MIDST OF WHAT YOU'RE GOING THROUGH?

When Anna focused her heart's attention on worshipping the Lord, she was able to see Jesus. Let's do the same—let's look to the One whom came **For All,** so we don't miss seeing Him this Christmas.

DOER OF THE WORD

How can you apply what you have learned from the Lord today?

_____

_____

_____

_____

SOCIAL CHALLENGE

// **WHAT IS SOMETHING YOU CAN SHARE ABOUT TODAY?**

// **STOP AND ASK GOD TO SHOW YOU WHO TO SHARE THIS WITH TODAY.**

// **WHO SHOULD YOU SHARE THIS WITH? (FINISH SENTENCE BELOW.)**

THIS MESSAGE IS _FOR ALL_ BUT IT IS ALSO FOR:

// **PRAY OVER THAT PERSON(S) OR GROUP AND ASK GOD FOR AN OPPORTUNITY AND COURAGE TO SHARE.**

IF YOU SHARE ON SOCIAL MEDIA
BE SURE TO USE #SACREDHOLIDAYS + TAG @SACREDHOLIDAYS.

FOR ALL

By Tia Plum

TALK TO GOD

PRAISE // REPENT // ASK // YIELD // STOP & LISTEN

As you sit down and open your study take a moment to reflect on how far you've come. Just 4 weeks ago was the start of a new beginning. Here you are today wrapping it up. Putting a big bow on the most beautiful gift you will ever receive or give. A Christmas story and promise FOR ALL. As you finish today, **savor it.** Listen to the pages of your Bible turning. It's a beautiful sound I've grown to love so much. Don't rush past the words you read today. Let them soak in deep. Praise God for the light He's revealed to you through His Word.

As a little girl, I fell deeply in love with words and books and the stories they tell. It feels bittersweet when I come to the last page of a good book. From cover to cover, every book has an ending; except one. The Bible. Yes, Revelation is the last chapter in the greatest story ever told. But the words and the promises of the gospel are without end. Jesus is **the only** Word from the beginning of ALL TIME that continues FOR ALL time.

   // **READ JOHN 1:1-5. WRITE OUT VERSES 1 & 2. CIRCLE EACH "THE WORD" AND "BEGINNING".**

When God repeats words in Scripture, we should look closely. This week you've been reading through John 1:1-14. Today we're going to look at John the Baptist who God sent to "bear witness" about Jesus, the light which was to come FOR ALL. The four gospels each speak of John's life and testimony. His ministry is important for us to consider. If you do a word search of **FOR ALL** you'll find 216 exact matches from Genesis 6:12-1Kings 3:15 in the ESV. As we've studied already, Old Testament prophecy points to the Messiah coming for all mankind. It directs us toward Jesus, The Word who became flesh and dwelt among us, full of grace and truth. John the Baptist "bore witness" about the deity of Jesus the Messiah, light in the darkness for all mankind. John's life and testimony are an example for us. In Acts 17:22-28, Paul proclaims that from the beginning of time, God has determined the time periods and places where all mankind will dwell so that all can seek God and find him. God has decided where every one of us will live and move and have our being, nothing is random or coincidence. Every detail of our lives is God's providence. We're here to prepare the way, bringing light to the darkness FOR ALL who've yet to seek or find him.

// LOOK UP THE WORD "WITNESS". WRITE THE DEFINITION AS IT APPLIES TO JOHN THE BAPTIST AND FOLLOWERS OF JESUS. WRITE IT HERE:

Witness is a key word in John's gospel; he uses the verb thirty-three times. Now, read John 1:14-18. Notice Verse 15. It says that John the Baptist _____out. He didn't just casually say these words. Scripture says he *cried* it out. Circle those words in your Bible as a reminder in the days and months to come.

// WHO HAS GOD PLACED IN YOUR LIFE THAT NEEDS YOU TO CRY OUT TO THEM ABOUT JESUS? HOW WILL YOU BEGIN TO SHOW AND TELL THEM ABOUT HIM?

Throughout this study we've seen that Jesus entered into the darkness of this world as light. *"The true light, which gives light to everyone, was coming into the world."* He came FOR ALL so that ALL could seek Him and find Him. He came for you and for every person He's put in your life in the ordinary places we live and visit day after day. Our "ordinary" lives offer "extraordinary" opportunities if we'll just choose them. Don't miss them. Don't miss the ones in front of you. The Christmas story that we've heard and studied is one we can't keep quietly to ourselves. It's full of grace, hope and love to be cried out FOR ALL to hear. What a privilege it is that God would use us in this way like John the Baptist. Don't lose the awe and wonder of the gospel. You don't *have* to be a voice. You *get* to be a voice. You may be the ONLY voice of truth and love crying out to those who feel lost in a wilderness. Use your voice gently, but in bold faith to point others to Jesus, our Messiah. The one who came to save us ALL.

// READ JOHN 1:6-8 AGAIN. FILL IN THE BLANK BELOW WITH YOUR NAME.

There was a woman sent from God, whose name was _____. She came as a witness to bear witness about the light that ALL might believe through her. She was not the light, but came to bear witness about the light.

// CLOSE YOUR TIME BY WRITING A PRAYER. THANK GOD FOR GIVING YOU A VOICE. ASK HIM TO PREPARE THE WAY FOR YOUR VOICE TO WITNESS ABOUT HIS LIGHT FOR ALL, TO ALL WHO NEED TO HEAR.

DOER OF THE WORD

How can you apply what you have learned from the Lord today?

_____

_____

_____

_____

SOCIAL CHALLENGE

// **WHAT IS SOMETHING YOU CAN SHARE ABOUT TODAY?**

// **STOP AND ASK GOD TO SHOW YOU WHO TO SHARE THIS WITH TODAY.**

// **WHO SHOULD YOU SHARE THIS WITH? (FINISH SENTENCE BELOW.)**

THIS MESSAGE IS _FOR ALL_ BUT IT IS ALSO FOR:

// **PRAY OVER THAT PERSON(S) OR GROUP AND ASK GOD FOR AN OPPORTUNITY AND COURAGE TO SHARE.**

IF YOU SHARE ON SOCIAL MEDIA
BE SURE TO USE #SACREDHOLIDAYS + TAG @SACREDHOLIDAYS.

LET'S
FRIE

STAY NDS

FOR GROUPS AND GROUP LEADERS

We were meant to live in connection and community with others. Let's gather together in groups to encourage, learn, listen, share, laugh, pray, and be women who are for one another during our holidays, and all the ordinary days in between.

Our hope is that we have a group (or more) meeting in each city in the United States. We know this is a crazy time of year for you but this is something that is so worth your time!

For more information on Groups, go to: sacredholidays.com/join-a-group

If you are interested in hosting a group, we think you are so awesome! We have a private Facebook group to support you, plus all kinds of free downloads to help you make your group awesome.

To sign your group up, go to: sacredholidays.com/host-a-group

ABOUT SACRED HOLIDAYS

Sacred Holidays

Helping you find less chaos and more Jesus during the holidays (and all the ordinary days in between).

Bible Studies and Books that bring you more Jesus!

Community through groups, social media, and more.

Resources to equip you for holidays big and small.

Fun, because loving God and others should be lots of fun!

SacredHolidays.com

#sacredholidays | @sacredholidays

Facebook.com/sacredholidays

Facebook.com/groups/SacredHolidaysTribe

BECKY KISER

Founder + CEO of Sacred Holidays and Author of For All

Becky is intent that women would fall in love with God's Word, then feel equipped and empowered to live it out. She believes that women can live out their own wild story, just like the ones we see of God's chosen in His Word, as they love Jesus and love people. She is the founder and CEO of Sacred Holidays—a ministry dedicated to helping women find less chaos and more Jesus during holidays through Bible study, community, resources, and lots of fun! She is determined to help women keep all the whimsy of the holidays, but help make them sacred—holy and set apart. Becky has a background in marketing and ministry, and is a certified Myers-Briggs life coach, bringing each of those experiences into her writing and speaking. Becky and her husband, Chris, live in The Woodlands, TX with their three girls.

Beckykiser.com | @beckykiser | facebook.com/becky.kiser

KELLY BOSCH | GROUP COORDINATOR & ALL THINGS AMAZING

Kelly wholeheartedly believes we are better together. In her mind, life is bolder and brighter when done with others. She is passionate about creating connections through shared experiences and authentic hospitality. Jesus modeled it, and Kelly thinks we should live it out. She gathers people together – whether around a decorated table, over pizza and paper plates, or in a social media group – because she believes every single person deserves to have a seat at the table. We all have a story to tell and she wants to know yours. While around her table, you can expect to hear about her love of story and her fondness for the Marvel Cinematic Universe. She is a lady geek, sports fanatic, adventure seeker, and expert gift giver. Her affection runs deep for smoked brisket, potatoes of any kind, cupcakes, and all things coconut. Kelly lives in the State of Hockey (also known as Minnesota) with her hard-working husband, Jeff, and energetic sons, Xander & Gavin.

@kellynbosch | facebook.com/kellynbosch

MOLLY PARKER | EDITOR

Molly Parker cherishes her role as contributor and editor for both Sacred Holidays and Anchored Press. In addition, she's a contributor for Crosswalk.com, where she weaves God's truth into everyday experiences. She's a toy designer's wife and mother of two teens and a young adult. Having lived in various cities and states, Molly has a heart for folks who miss "home." When she's not french-braiding hair or scolding her basset hound, she's either eating cake, baking a cake, or thinking about cake, which is surprising considering she's worked in the fitness industry 25 years.

@mollyjeanparker | facebook.com/molly.parker.507

MEGAN SJUTS WITH BUILDING 07 | STUDY DESIGNER

Megan Sjuts is the owner of Building 07 and designer for Sacred Holidays. Her mission as a designer is to simplify the design process and serve creative professionals and business owners. Building 07 offers a full range of professional design services that cover the gamut of graphic to web design, and all the creative strategy in between.

When she is not behind the screen designing for clients, she is teaching graphic design courses at Rogue Community College in Southern Oregon, where she lives with her husband, Elliot, their chocolate lab, Dixie, and four chickens, Sunny, Popcorn, Peanut and Penny.

@building07 | Building07.com

MEET THE CONTRIBUTORS

MANDY ARIOTO | ZECHARIAH

Mandy Arioto is the President and CEO of MOPS International. She and her husband Joe, live in Denver, Colorado with their three awesome kids. Her new book, *Have More Fun* launches in April 2019. In the meantime, listen to her podcast found at mandyarioto.com.

Mandyarioto.com | @mandyarioto | facebook.com/mandy.mcavoyarioto

KAT ARMSTRONG | BETHLEHEM

Kat Armstrong (MA, Christian Education) was born in Houston, TX where the humidity ruins her curls. She is a powerful voice in our generation as an innovative ministry leader and sought-after communicator and a Harper Collins author. As the co-founder and Executive Director of Polished Ministries, an outreach that gathers young professional women to navigate career and explore faith together, she has been invested in the lives of women for a decade sharing the gospel. Kat and her husband Aaron have been married for fifteen years, live in Dallas, TX with their son Caleb and attend Dallas Bible Church where Aaron serves as the lead pastor.

katarmstrong.com | @katarmstrong1 | facebook.com/kat.teamarmstrong

JENN JETT BARRETT | ELIZABETH

Jenn Jett Barrett is a dreamer, a doer and a champion of risk takers. When she is not running her design business, she is encouraging women through her community and retreat, Camp Well – a place where dreamers and doers who are weary and overwhelmed can come and be reminded of who God called them to be and walk confidently in that calling. Her faith has been tested time and again and proves the incredible power of the resurrection and the freedom that comes through it. Her heart is that we would all claim the same power and freedom available to us and that we would choose obedience over outcome.

Jennjett.com | @jenn_jett | facebook.com/JennJett123

LINDSAY BENEDETTO | NO ROOM & THE MANGER

Lindsay is a coach's wife, mom to four littles, and the Director of Development & Operations for Polished Ministries. She is passionate about sharing the stories of young professional women who have been impacted by Polished while inviting others to join their efforts in engaging culture with the gospel. When not playing dollhouse with her girls or spending time with her hubby, Lindsay enjoys being active, reading, and coffee dates (none of which happen often during this season of life).

@lindsay_benedetto | facebook.com/lindsaybenedetto

HEATHER BOCK | ANGELS

Heather is a new Texan, a homeschooling, running, party planning, and teaching mother of three with a degree focused on Biblical studies, literature, and French. She wrote a Bible study called Glimpses of Jesus in Genesis, and she writes posts every week on her blog, Glimpses of Jesus.

Glimpsesofjesus.com | @heather.bock | facebook.com/heather.bock

AMBER BURGER | THE HOLY SPIRIT

Amber is married to Vernon and together they are raising Titus and Justus. They are expecting another son due this winter while also pursuing adoption of a daughter from South Sudan. Amber and Vernon founded and run His Voice Global, a nonprofit providing food, shelter, education, and hope to children and families in South Sudan, Uganda, Kenya . . . and beyond. While working for His Voice, Amber homeschools her boys, writes, leads worship, fights human trafficking in cities across the globe and teaches women to love and lead well in their homes and communities. Amber is a life and wellness coach in her spare time as she loves helping women be their healthiest self. Amber is smart, creative and downright fun to be around. She loves books, food, a good late night and an even better cup of coffee. On any given day you'll find her house filled with friends and she wouldn't have it any other way!

facebook.com/amberburger | @amberburger

CHRISTINA CRENSHAW | JOSEPH

Dr. Christina Crenshaw is a professor, researcher, writer, and human trafficking fighter. She teaches writing and vocational leadership courses as a full time Lecturer at Baylor University. She is also a post doctoral fellow at Dallas Theological Seminary's Hendricks Center. Christina is a strong believer in faith based cultural engagement and leadership; she believes The Church is the answer to many of the world's questions and needs. She researches human trafficking prevention education, a subject on which she frequently speaks. She has worked with several anti human trafficking organizations such as The A21 Campaign, UnBound Now, The Heart of Texas Human Trafficking Coalition, and Operation Mobilization's Freedom Climb. In addition to her human trafficking work, Christina speaks on vocational leadership, which equips Christians to discover their calling and then lead in their sphere of influence. From 2015-2016, Christina served on Propel Women's Brain Trust during its launch year. Prior to moving to Waco, TX, she lived in Southern California and held an Assistant Professor position at California Baptist University. Christina earned a PhD in Education with an emphasis in English literature from Baylor University. She and her husband of 15 years are raising two beautiful, wild boys.

drchristinacrenshaw.com | @Christina_Crenshaw

MELANIE DALE | THE FIRST SEVEN DAYS

Melanie Dale is a minivan mama and total weirdo who stinks at small talk. Her laugh is a combination honk-snort, and it's so bad that people have moved away from her in the movie theater. She adores sci-fi and superheroes and is terrified of Pinterest. Author of Women Are Scary: The Totally Awkward Adventure of Finding Mom Friends and It's Not Fair: Learning to Love the Life You Didn't Choose, she's also a monthly contributor for Coffee+Crumbs, and her essays are featured in their book, The Magic of Motherhood. She's a panelist for MomsEveryday TV, an advocate for Children's HopeChest, and a speaker for churches, conferences, and events across the country. Living in the Atlanta area, she enjoys recording her podcast, Lighten Up with Melanie Dale, blogging at Unexpected.org, and raising her three kids from three different continents.

Unexpected.org | @unexpectedmel | facebook.com/unexpectedmel

JANDI HARRIS | MARY

Jandi, born and raised in Liberia, West Africa, is passionate about fostering a Christian community that encourages and uplifts women as they grow in their relationship with Christ. Jandi draws inspiration from her experience as a wife, mother, high school educator, and an ordained minister to shape her blog, Broken for Building. She believes that God uses all parts of our beautiful, yet sometimes broken lives to build us into Kingdom warriors. When she is not writing, journaling, or trying to win the war against laundry, you can find her at her sewing machine. She lives in the Atlanta area with her husband, Oliver and their three daughters.

brokenforbuilding.com // facebook.com/brokenforbuilding // @brokenforbuilding

ELIZABETH HYNDMAN | GENEALOGY

Elizabeth Hyndman is a writer, editor, and social media strategist. She lives in Nashville, TN and loves chai lattes and the Oxford comma. She blogs occasionally at edhyndman.com.

Edhyndman.com | @edhyndman

KARA-KAE JAMES | ADAM AND EVE

Kara-Kae James desires to see women walk in their full potential as moms, wives and daughters of Christ. Her book, *Mom Up*, will hit shelves January of 2019 to encourage moms to seek abundance in motherhood! She is the founder and Executive Director of Thrive Moms, a ministry dedicated to empowering moms. She's married to her husband, Brook, and together they are raising their four children, and are passionate about adoption and creatively reaching people for Jesus.

karakaejames.com | @karakae.james | facebook.com/karakae.james

RACHEL JOY | SHEPHERDS

Rachel Joy is a mom of four, a pastor's wife, and Founder and Director of Sparrow Conference- a catalytic gathering connecting young women to Jesus, the Bible, one another and the local church. She has lead and taught Bible studies for over fifteen years. Rachel's passion is to see young women come to the powerful, saving grace and knowledge of Jesus Christ and be on mission as reconcilers. It is her joy to point to Jesus because in Him alone do we find truth, freedom, identity and purpose. Rachel describes her life as busy, loud, crazy and she absolutely loves it! You will often find her drinking far too much coffee, having a dance party with her little ones, writing for fun and having a good, long dinner with folks from church or the neighborhood. Rachel calls The Village Church in Highland Village, Texas home.

Sparrowwomen.com | @rachelrjoy

KELLY D. KING | WISE MEN

Kelly D. King is the Women's Ministry Specialist for LifeWay Christian Resources. She is an author and blogger who encourages and equips women to lead in their passion and calling. She holds a Master of Theology degree from Gateway Seminary.

lifeway.com/womensministry | @kellydking | facebook.com/kellykennedyking

SHARON MILLER | PROPHECIES

Sharon Hodde Miller is an author, speaker, pastor's wife, and mom, with a PhD on women and calling. She blogs at SheWorships.com, and is the author of *Free of Me: Why Life Is Better When It's Not about You.*

Sheworships.com | @sharonhmiller | facebook.com/sharonhoddemiller

OSHETA MOORE | SIMEON

My name is Osheta. It's pronounced, "O-she-da" and so many people have asked if it means something. It doesn't. My dad just made it up. But if I were to go to Urban Dictionary and create a definition for my name it might say something like this: An ENFJ mama who loves parties, people, and popcorn with red wine. A pastor's wife who is convinced God has a sense of humor. A Peacemaker who loves Jesus a lot and cusses... a little. An optimistic cookbook reader. A hopeless romantic. A goofball with a little bit of sass.

Shalominthecity.com | @oshetam | facebook.com/ShalomintheCity

MOLLY PARKER | KING HEROD AND SCRIBES

Molly Parker cherishes her role as contributor and editor for Anchored Press Devotional Planners and for Sacred Holidays Bible studies and resources. She also regularly writes for Crosswalk.com ghostwrites for various clientele. Molly is a toy designer's wife and mother of two teens and a young adult. Having lived in various cities and states, Molly has a heart for folks who miss "home." When she's not French-braiding hair or scolding her basset hound, she's eating cake, baking a cake, or thinking about cake, which is surprising considering she's worked in the fitness industry 25 years.

@mollyjeanparker | facebook.com/molly.parker.507

TIA PLUM | FOR ALL

I've found my greatest joy in loving Jesus, abiding in His Word and doing what He says. I've been married to my lifetime love and biggest encourager, David, for 28 years. We treasure being mom & dad to our adult daughters, Mackenzie & Madisen. In my "empty nest season" I have a deepening desire to run the race God has set before me advancing the Gospel and literacy for the sake of Bible literacy among the marginalized at home and in the world—especially Africa.

@tiaplum

REBECCA RENFROW | MARY'S SONG AND TREASURE

Rebecca is a wife, mom to two fun teenage boys, and a business and life coach. She is passionate about helping the mom entrepreneur grow her business and raise her kids with purpose by increasing productivity, reach her goals and keep her priorities as a mom and business owner intact. She is also the co-host of the podcast Story Cast. Story Cast gives women a stage to share their unique stories. The mission of Story Cast is to show women that they can be confident in who God made them to be, to live life to the fullest and to embrace each small and big moment given, and to realize their stories matter. When Rebecca isn't stuck in the car transporting her boys and all their friends back and forth to activities, you might find her on a jog around the lake in her neighborhood or on a coffee date with her best girlfriends.

Rebeccarenfrow.com | @rebeccarenfrow | facebook.com/RebeccaRenfrowBiz

SHARIFA STEVENS | JESUS

A New York native, Sharifa earned a bachelor of arts degree from Columbia University before moving to Dallas, Texas, where she received a master of theology degree from Dallas Theological Seminary. She is a writer and aspiring sleeper. Sharifa contributed to the book Vindicating the Vixens: Revisiting Sexualized, Vilified, & Marginalized Women of the Bible. Sharifa is wife to a Renaissance man and mother to two lively boys.

Sharifastevens.com | @sharifawrites | facebook.com/sharifahaylestevens

JEN WEAVER | ANNA

Jen Weaver is the author of A Wife's Secret to Happiness and is passionate about sharing strength with others as a Bible teacher, speaker, and blogger at thejenweaver.com. Married to her best friend Jared, she's the happy mom of a growing family.

Thejenweaver.com | @thejenweaver | facebook.com/thejenweaverpage

10% FOR VULNERABLE WOMEN AND CHILDREN IN KENYA (LEARN MORE!) OUR PARTNERSHIP WITH HIS VOICE GLOBAL

His Voice Global (HVG) is called to work in areas of the world with high populations of vulnerable women and children to partner with local leaders to fulfill their vision to care for, educate, and encourage the vulnerable women and children in their area. We currently have partnerships in South Sudan, Kenya and Uganda.

Sacred Holidays specifically partners with our work in Kenya. HVG works in a city in which prostitution and the commercial sex trade industry dominates the economy. Women and children, both by force and by choice, work the streets in order to feed and house themselves and their children. We are partnered with a local Kenyan church called Rift Valley Fellowship (RVF). RVF staff works tirelessly to help these women and children get off the streets and into affordable homes and integrity filled jobs. We have a boys and a girls home, providing holistic restoration including safety, education, counseling, and over all physical care. As children come into our care, we work closely with their mothers through a ministry to the women called Women of Courage. Women of Courage exist to love, provide, disciple, and train women in trades that they can eventually support themselves.

HOW YOU CAN HELP!

First, you already have! You purchasing this study has provided funds for this work!

- ☐ If you'd like to do more, there are so many ways you can help advocate for these beautiful women and children in Kenya.

- ☐ Educate yourself. Hear the stories and the needs. Follow His Voice Global on social media: @hisvoiceglobal and facebook.com/hisvoice. Also, learn lots more and sign up for our newsletter so that you can grow as an advocate for these vulnerable women and children in Kenya at www.hisvoiceglobal.com

- ☐ Support a child by giving them an education: For an Elementary and Middle School study it is $165 a year, or just $14 a month. For High School students it's $600 a year, or $50 a month. This sacrifice on your part is what will change the future of that kids life!

- ☐ Support a mother as she chooses to stay off the streets: $135 a month to provide a home, food, hygiene items, clothing, and job support.

- ☐ Provide a week worth of food for our feeding program that keeps kids from working the street in order to eat. It also pays to feeds everyone in the Recovery program on Saturdays and anyone who comes to church on Sunday, often their only meal/meals of the weekend. $170 a week. We know this is a larger expense, so grab a few friends and go into this together if this isn't something you could do on your own.

☐ Sign up to go to Kenya or Uganda with our teams! Contact amber@hisvoiceglobal.com for more information on our trips.

☐ Become a monthly partner of His Voice Global! There are countless needs to come up to support the work being done in Kenya. By giving generally you allow there to be resources for the local church to meet the needs of the people as they arise.

☐ Host an advocacy night in your home. Grab 10 or so (or more!) of your friends and host a night in your home where they can learn about His Voice Global. We will provide you with video or a staff member to come and share. This can look any way you want it! You can have it low key or super to-do! During the halftime of a big game, or an entire dinner and program. Contact amber@hisvoiceglobal.com and she will make it happen! We can brainstorm together what would be the most fun and best fit for your people.

P.S. from Becky

Ladies, I cannot encourage you enough to do something, anything. I endorse very few ministries because I want you to know the things I push you to be a part of are worth your time, doing real work, and being good stewards of your funds. I have been to Kenya now twice and have known Amber and Vernon, the founders of this ministry for nearly two decades—they and this ministry are the real deal. I have stood in the homes of women who were once prostituting themselves all throughout the day just to provide a bite to eat for the week for their family. But God. He has used HVG and RVF to bring about His redemption story.

FOLLOW HIS VOICE GLOBAL ON SOCIAL MEDIA!

Instagram: @hisvoiceglobal | Facebook: His Voice Global

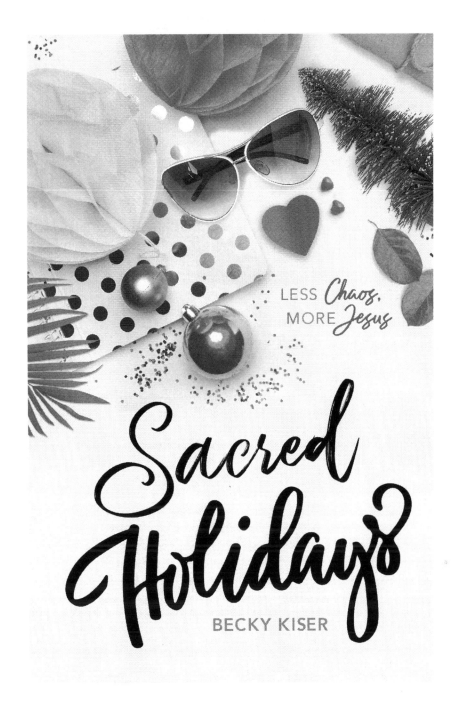

**EXCERPT FROM SACRED HOLIDAYS: LESS CHAOS, MORE JESUS
BY BECKY KISER**

Available where books are sold online:

978-1-5359-1412-3

Published by B&H Publishing Group
Nashville, Tennessee

Dewey Decimal Classification: 394.2
Subject Heading: HOLIDAYS \ STRESS (PSYCHOLOGY) \
FAMILY TRADITIONS

Published in association with D.C. Jacobson & Associates, LLC,
an Author Management Company, www. dcjacobson.com.

Unless otherwise noted, Scripture is taken from the English
Standard Version. ESV® Text Edition: 2016. Copyright © 2001 by
Crossway Bibles, a publishing ministry of Good News Publishers.

Also used: *The Message* (MSG), copyright © 1993, 1994, 1995,
1996, 2000, 2001, 2002 by Eugene H. Peterson

Also used: New Living Translation (NLT), copyright © 1996,
2004, 2015 by Tyndale House Foundation. Used by permission
of Tyndale House Publishers, Inc., Carol Stream, Illinois 60188.
All rights reserved.

Also used: New International Version®, NIV® Copyright
©1973, 1978, 1984, 2011 by Biblica, Inc.® Used
by permission. All rights reserved worldwide.

Cover design by Studio Nth.
Author photo © Amanda Liberto.

1 2 3 4 5 6 7 • 21 20 19 18

CONTENTS

How to Use This Book *(because it's different than other books you've read)* 1

PART 1: LESS CHAOS, MORE JESUS (READ NOW)

Chapter 1 | Regrets, Better Ways, and Baby Steps 13
Chapter 2 | Social Experiments and All Things Whimsy 27

PART 2: HOLIDAYS (READ 30–60 DAYS BEFORE HOLIDAY)

Chapter 3 | New Year's 39
Chapter 4 | Valentine's Day 57
Chapter 5 | Lent and Easter 69
Chapter 6 | Summer 85
Chapter 7 | Halloween 101
Chapter 8 | Thanksgiving 115
Chapter 9 | Advent and Christmas 125
Chapter 10 | Happy Birthday 147

PART 3: COMMON STRUGGLES (READ AS NEEDED)

Chapter 11 | How to Not Be *THAT* Christian 159
Chapter 12 | Realistic Expectations 171
Chapter 13 | Conflict, Drama, and All the Feels 181
Chapter 14 | Budgets and Generosity 197
Chapter 15 | Schedules and Plans 209
Chapter 16 | Grief 217
Chapter 17 | Santa and the Easter Bunny 229
Chapter 18 | P.S.: Be Yourself and Be with Others 237

Acknowledgments 239

HOW TO USE
THIS BOOK

BECAUSE IT'S DIFFERENT THAN OTHER BOOKS YOU'VE READ

Holidays can be crazy. And because you're holding this book in your hands, I think you'd agree. I love that about you—you are willing to face crazy head-on and do something about it. Holidays can be especially tricky to navigate as a Christian—wanting to celebrate and focus on Christ yet being pulled into the chaos or whimsy of each holiday.

You aren't alone; nearly every woman I talk to struggles with this. You don't have to stay in the same cycle of wishing things would be different. Jesus called us to not just live, but to live abundantly (John 10:10). This is the beginning of a new way of doing holidays—one that involves less chaos, more Jesus, and not getting too caught up in the holiday whimsy or magical festivities, nor overwhelmed by the holiday chaos.

I am so proud of you for getting this book! You're about to begin a journey to making holidays more sacred—holy and set apart! This book is laid out a little different than most books you've read before, so I wanted to walk you through how to use it.

WHAT THIS BOOK MEANS BY "SACRED"

Throughout this book, you'll hear me say a phrase over and over: "sacred—holy and set apart." Before we go any further, let me tell you what I mean by that phrase. I'm breaking up your approach to the holidays into two categories.

First, *holy*. I want to help your holidays become holy or *dedicated* to Christ (and others). Instead of getting lost in the way the culture does holidays (making it all about self or about applause you could receive for pulling off a perfect event), I want us to get lost in the reality that Christ gave us these holidays to enjoy, and that we can worship Him in the middle of all the whimsy. Even if a holiday isn't a direct celebration of Christ Himself, we can still put Christ and others at the center of all our celebratory moments instead of ourselves! While we don't want to over-spiritualize every single moment, sometimes we can be guilty of under-spiritualizing, can't we? Part of my mission in this book is to help you find more Jesus in each holiday, making it more holy for you, your family, and your friends.

Second, *set apart*. While we certainly want to make the holidays more about Jesus, we don't have to believe the lie that spiritual means impractical. Sometimes we need help setting apart a holiday from the rest of the calendar year, making it special with intentional planning. The "set apart" portion of the holiday chapters are simply there to help you be more intentional about your holiday habits in really practical ways.

As you'll see in each of the chapters that deal with specific holidays, I give you ideas about both of these categories. If you struggle with following in the culture's footsteps and forgetting the spiritual side of the holidays, lost in a sea of Pinterest activities and exhaustion, you'll see some ideas on how to make your holiday more holy, helping you get more Jesus! On the flip side, if you struggle with over-spiritualizing the holidays to the point of never even getting to practical ways of having fun, you'll also see some fun ideas on how to make your holiday "set apart" from the mundane of everyday life with whimsical activities and intentional plans. Sometimes during the crazy of celebration seasons, we need to pull away for more Jesus. Other times we need to bust out the planner, take the bull by the horns, and get intentional about our holiday planning so that we can look back and say it was truly set apart from the rest of the year in practical and fun ways. This book doesn't make you choose; it will help you make your holidays more holy *and* set apart.

THIS BOOK IS MEANT TO STAY OUT

I don't mean stays out in that pile of books you hope to read that crowd up your nightstand, taunting you from your shelves, unread. This book is one you keep within easy reach because you will want to reference it throughout the year. This book of yours is meant to be a companion that guides you through all holidays—not just the big ones. If we can change how we approach the holidays, our lives will be so much more free and full—and headed toward abundant living!

This past year I started keeping my planner on the counter, opened to the current day. By placing my planner out where I could see it each day, it radically changed my perspective on all the things I was juggling. I felt less overwhelmed and more in control than ever. I approached life with more intention and reached more goals than I ever could have imagined. I was able to say no to more things because I was able to see that I simply could not make them fit. I became a better follower of Jesus, wife, mom, friend, teacher, writer, boss, and neighbor. Don't get me wrong, I still have a long way to go. But this simple step of putting my planner out was a game changer.

What if you did the same thing with your holidays? What if instead of waiting to think about them right before they happen, or regretting afterward that you didn't approach them with more intention, you were prepared a month or two in advance? Let's stop living life in survival mode, constantly on the defense, a victim of our schedules and the expectations of others. Instead, let's live sacred—holy and set apart—with our holidays having less chaos, and more Jesus.

THIS BOOK IS MEANT TO BE READ IN STAGES

This book is broken up into three sections:

PART 1: LESS CHAOS, MORE JESUS

(READ RIGHT AWAY)

I know you want to quickly get to the meat of this book, the holiday chapters, where you'll receive practical insights for how you can make your holidays sacred. However, we must deal with our heart and our approach to holidays first. This section is to help set the stage for what it truly means to have less chaos and more Jesus during the holidays. Make time to read these two chapters before you begin the holiday chapters.

Before we get busy "doing," I want to remind you about the story of Mary and Martha in Luke 10. I think sometimes Martha gets a bad rap from her interaction with Jesus inside her home. Oftentimes she is portrayed as this frantic, bitter, workaholic woman, and the truth is, we just don't know that about her character. Sometimes I wonder if she was just like you and me—simply wanting to serve others and Jesus. Like her, we want to create this culture and way of life that brings God glory and others lots of joy. However—and this is a big however—we get lost in our doing and we just need to stop. Mary stopped and was found simply sitting at Jesus' feet, listening to what He had to say. Then we learn the real problem with Martha wasn't that she was serving but that she was *distracted* in her serving (v. 40). Jesus replied in verses 41–42, "Martha, Martha, you are anxious and troubled about many things, but one thing is necessary. Mary has chosen the good portion, which will not be taken away from her."

In Part 1 we will focus on the good portion before we focus on the tasks of carrying things out. Obviously, Martha had to work or else no one would eat. The problem wasn't in her working; it was in being so distracted she missed the good portion. Let's not miss it by being so distracted in our attempts to make holidays sacred. Let's first sit, listen, and learn. Then we can set the table and make the meal, but let's not be distracted by those first.

PART 2: HOLIDAYS

(READ 30–60 DAYS BEFORE HOLIDAYS)

You can certainly read Part 2 right away, but 30–60 days prior to each holiday, refer back to this section in order to receive the most continual benefit. Here you will find the following in each chapter:

- Encouragement in living sacred during this holiday.
- A little historical—cultural and/or religious—context.
- Write your personal mission statement or hope for that holiday.
- Ideas for all women to live sacred during each holiday.
- Ideas for the kiddos in our lives to live sacred too. *(Note: this isn't just for moms; see the section below to be reminded that this book is for every type of person, single, married, with kids, or otherwise, not just parents!)*
- Journaling space for you to record what's worked and what hasn't worked.
- Journaling space for you to record any ideas you can try in the future.

Go ahead and schedule your alerts on your calendar to prepare for each holiday. Set them as an annual recurring event. If you aren't able to make that appointment to plan, then commit to reschedule it for a better time. Since you are scheduling your holiday prep-time a year or more in advance, you will have to make adjustments. However, a simple reminder will increase the chances that you will make the time to sit down.

Check the box below after you've put the session on your calendar for each holiday:

- ❑ New Year's (schedule in November or December)
- ❑ Valentine's Day (Schedule in December or January)
- ❑ Lent and Easter (Schedule in January or February)
- ❑ Summer (Schedule in April or May)
- ❑ Halloween (Schedule in August or September)
- ❑ Thanksgiving (Schedule September or October)
- ❑ Advent and Christmas (Schedule in October or November)
- ❑ Happy Birthday (Schedule in _____)

PART 3: COMMON STRUGGLES

(READ AS NEEDED)

Finally, decide which common struggles you would benefit from reading. You might find it helpful to read through each of those chapters now, so you've learned what they have to teach you. Then come back to them as a refresher before the holidays hit. Know that your needs for each of these chapters will change year after year, hence the reason to keep this book within easy reach at all times.

THIS BOOKS IS MEANT TO GET MESSY

This resource was written for interaction. I view it as part book/part resource, in hopes that you no longer have to search the Internet for hours and hours to try to find what may or may not work for you. I have included some of the best practices for holidays—both the internal processing and prep that you'll find in Part 1 and in each of the holiday chapters from Part 2. However, there are many opportunities for you to process things out in this book. I will give you prompts and ask you questions, providing space for you to answer. Use this space; don't keep your pages clean. The more you interact with this book and make it your resource, the more sacred—holy and set apart—your holidays will become.

I have a sign that hangs at the bottom of my stairs that reads, "Pardon the mess but my children are making memories." I have it hanging there as a joke for others to read before they enter the war zone that can be our upstairs family room and my girls' shared bedroom. No matter how hard we try to clean or how many chore charts I hang, that space is always a mess. That sign reminds me each time I go upstairs that the messes are memories that my girls are making. I don't want them to live in a home with plastic coverings over our furniture or dishes they are afraid to touch. I want them to live in our home and make a ton of memories in it.

I have the same hope for you, my friend. This book is yours and I want you to make a mess with it. The more messes you make in it, the more memories you will have.

THIS BOOK IS MEANT FOR EVERYONE (NOT JUST PARENTS!)

I was very hesitant to include ideas for kids in this book for two reasons. First, I didn't want any person who wasn't a parent to feel like this book wasn't for them. It is so for you! It is for every person. The truth is, most of us have kids in our lives in some capacity—we are aunts, teachers, volunteers, grandparents, friends with moms, etc. These ideas I list are for anyone with a kid in their life, which is pretty much anyone! The hope is that we will all find ways to help train up children to have a more sacred approach to the holidays.

Second, I do not want parents to make holidays all about their kids. This is probably the number one question I get with Sacred Holidays, the ministry: "How can I help my kids learn more about Jesus during the holidays?" I love the heart of these parents so much, and I so get it. And as a ministry leader, I know I could be far more "successful" if I were to monopolize on this desire. The problem is, even though the intent is beautiful, the approach can be imbalanced. The best analogy I have for this is how the flight attendant says that we must first put our oxygen masks on and then help the child. For our children to have the best chance at life, we must first take care of ourselves. This is hard for us as moms because we will do just about anything for our kids. However, and this is a really big however, our goal is not to raise little Christian robots; our aim is to make disciples of Christ. But every disciple needs a discipler, someone showing them the way, not just telling them what to do (or programming their robot to do the right thing). We must show our kids the way by living the sacred way ourselves.

This book is a timeless resource for you, regardless of what season of life you find yourself.

THIS BOOK IS MEANT TO BE EXPERIENCED ALONGSIDE OTHERS

We can't force others to change their approach to holidays, and that is never our aim. However, we can invite others on the journey toward making our holidays sacred—holy and set apart. The truth is, most of your friends and family members want the same thing you do! They want less chaos. And if they are believers, they want more Jesus too! If they are not, they probably do want the abundant life Jesus could offer through the holidays, but they simply have been searching for solutions in the wrong places. Christian or not, they all want to feel like they are living abundantly during the holidays, not caught up in the whimsy and survival-mode-crazy of it. So let's invite them to join us.

We know that we do better when we do things with others—there is power in numbers. It's the reason why weight-loss programs and workout places that promote group gatherings and accountability models are so successful. When we have others who are trying to make the same kind of changes we are, we do better.

We learn from their ways—what has worked and not worked. We have accountability to follow through. We discover more fun or efficient ways of doing things. We hear "me too" instead of assuming we're the only ones struggling with something. Plus, it's just a whole lot more fun!

Who are some people you could invite on this journey with you?

Send them a text message telling them what you are doing and invite them to join you! Put a check next to their name or cross it off once you've reached out to them.

Also, be sure to check out the Sacred Holidays website (sacredholidays.com) for other ways to build connection and community with our tribe of people, plus our team.

ARE YOU READY?

Okay, let's do this! Let's find less chaos and more Jesus in the holidays ahead! Let's make your holidays more sacred—holy and set apart. And let's find some freedom from common struggles that get the best of us too often.

We'd love to hear from you if you're on board, so we can follow along with your journey and our whole tribe can learn from you (our own virtual group). As you learn things or try things, be sure to tag @sacredholidays and use #sacredholidays in your posts, so we can all learn from and celebrate with one another. We are in this together!

PART 1

LESS
Chaos,
MORE
Jesus

(READ NOW)

CHAPTER 1

REGRETS, BETTER WAYS, AND BABY STEPS

This is the beginning of a new way for you—a new season of making holidays more sacred—holy and set apart. You should be really proud of yourself that you are taking the time to learn about this and actually making some changes. It's worth it; I can promise you that right now. This will not be easy, but, friend, it is so worth it and you can do this.

How many times have we talked to older women and heard, "I wish I would've done or known that when I was your age"? Let's learn from the women who are ahead of us and choose a different way, the one they wish they would've chosen (the one that still isn't too late for you, if you would consider yourself to be the older woman). We can choose this way when we are twenty-two, thirty-six, forty-four, fifty-nine, sixty-seven, and older. We are never too old for this! Let's not live a life of wishing we would've done something. Starting today, let's live the life we were meant to live—free from regrets and taking one baby step at a time toward a better way!

Holidays have become this imbalanced juxtaposition of chaos and whimsy. We are stressed by the shopping and thrilled by the look on the faces of the ones we spoiled. We are exhausted by the parties yet so excited to get all dressed up to celebrate the day or the person. We are easily irritated by our families and absolutely smitten at the same time. We hate ourselves for eating more than we should yet cannot get enough home cooking and treats. And we're torn between our love for all things whimsical and our deep desire to celebrate Jesus in each of the holidays.

The last one is the hardest, wouldn't you agree? We love Jesus and want to follow Him, yet we struggle to make the holidays about Him. We are stuck doing things the way they've always been done. We are stuck celebrating just as the world celebrates. We are stuck celebrating the way our family has always done it before or the way picture-perfect posts on social media have told us to over the years. The idea of something new, even something sacred, feels a bit overwhelming.

REGRETS

We all have regrets when it comes to the holidays, and oftentimes it's the shame of these regrets that keeps us from thinking we are even capable of a better way.

My biggest regret during all the holidays is how I inevitably default to the thirteen-year-old version of myself. When it was New Year's, I used to set big (and unrealistic) goals for myself, resolutions that lasted all of a week. On Valentine's Day, I was more concerned about who was showing me love than loving others (and chocolate, really it's about the chocolate). During Easter, it seemed to be more about the dress (priorities!). Summer can be a whirl of trying to have as much fun as possible. Halloween feels like a slightly rebellious thing to participate in as a Christian. Thanksgiving is the physical proof I turned thirteen when I'm surrounded by every member of my family. Christmas, while a celebration of Jesus' coming, can easily be overshadowed by wish lists and events. And my birthday never quite seems to measure up to the expectation in my head.

I'm a mess. We all are. We feel like we should have it all figured out by now and don't understand why we don't.

What Regrets Surround These Holidays?

Ask your Father to remind you of holiday-related regrets. Give yourself time to really process this today. Then, remember that this is your book, your resource for years and years to come. So come back to this page each year and you can add to the list below. The reason why we want to name the regrets is because we want to clearly and specifically identify the things we do not want to continue. There is no shame in naming it. (Tip: be general only when it's referring to someone else. Sometimes it's best to just use the first letter of a name or a place, to keep this page confidential.)

NEW YEAR'S:

_____

_____

VALENTINE'S DAY:

_____

_____

LENT AND EASTER:

_____

_____

SUMMER:

_____

_____

HALLOWEEN:

_____

_____

THANKSGIVING:

_____

_____

ADVENT AND CHRISTMAS:

_____

_____

HAPPY BIRTHDAY (INCLUDING YOUR BIRTHDAY AND OTHERS):

_____

_____

BETTER WAYS

We women are masters at staying in shame longer than we should, but shame has never been ours to carry. I'm a total word nerd and absolutely love the dictionary (and translation dictionaries). _Merriam-Webster's_ dictionary defines shame as "a painful emotion caused by consciousness of guilt, shortcoming, or impropriety. A condition of humiliating disgrace or disrepute. Something that brings censure or reproach; something to be regretted."

We just made a long list of regrets, which can tempt us to fall right back into that trap of shame, leading to guilt. We are vastly aware of our shortcomings. Holidays are so sweet and so magical in so many contexts, but we have so many regrets. So we settle into shame and believe there is no better way.

Before we move on to a better way of approaching the holidays, we must clearly identify what is true and what is a lie. What is true is all the things you listed above. We all have regrets about past holidays—wishing that certain elements were different. Identifying each one helps us learn. But the lie becomes evident when we take on shame, which isn't from your Father in heaven. John 8:44 speaks into this concept, "He [the devil] was a murderer from the beginning, and does not stand in the truth, because there is no truth in him. When he lies, he speaks out of his character, for he is a liar and the father of lies."

The father of lies, Satan, slithers right up next to the list of regrets we just processed and tells you, "Things will never change." He leads you to believe you will never get this right. He reminds you of others who have it all together (at least on their social media feed) and puts you in your place. He even tells you what a failure you are for not worshiping Jesus more during the holidays—holidays that are supposed to be about Him. He is the one who puts fear in us around holidays like Halloween or Christmas, causing more fear of the world than a love for others. Being a follower of Jesus in this day is so very complicated, and the enemy is taking every opportunity to slither up next to us and whisper lies in our ears, just as he did to Eve in the garden (Gen. 3).

When we look at our list of regrets above, we can listen to one of two voices: the voice of truth or the voice of lies. Jesus said in John 10:10, "The thief comes only to steal and kill and destroy. I come that they may have life and have it abundantly." I love how *The Message* translation by Eugene Peterson words this verse, "I came so they can have real and eternal life, more and better life than they ever dreamed of."

Yes! Isn't this what you want, my friend? Isn't this why you picked up this book? You believe there is a better way. You believe there must be a way "more and better than you ever dreamed of."

A New and Better Way

Just as we listed our regrets about the holidays, I want you to make a new and "better way" list. This list depicts what could be—and dreams about what you wish and hope would happen during the holidays. Don't over-spiritualize this either. Keep the traditions and cultural whimsy that are good and life-giving. Then ask your Father what might be a better way.

NEW YEAR'S:

_____

_____

VALENTINE'S DAY:

_____

_____

LENT AND EASTER:

_____

_____

SUMMER:

_____

_____

HALLOWEEN:

_____

_____

THANKSGIVING:

_____

_____

ADVENT AND CHRISTMAS:

_____

_____

**HAPPY BIRTHDAY (INCLUDING YOUR
BIRTHDAY AND OTHERS):**

_____

_____

I wish I could sit across from you now and hear these dreams God is creating in you. I know our tendency is to buffer our dreams just in case they don't come about. Here is what I want to encourage you to do, sweet friend: dream without the safety net. Abundant life in Jesus, as we defined earlier, is "more and better than they (that's you!) ever dreamed."

One of my favorite verses in all the Scriptures is the reality check that He is God and we are not, that is found in Isaiah 55:8–9, "For my thoughts are not your thoughts, neither are your ways my ways, declares the Lord. For as the heavens are higher than the earth, so are my ways higher than your ways and my thoughts your thoughts." Our Father takes such delight in our dreams and our faith. The reason why I love dreaming and planning is because it's part of the first steps of faith; it's our acknowledgment that there is actually a better way.

Then our Father takes it from there. He took Noah's first step and used him to build an ark. He took Moses—yes, the fearful-and-afraid-to-speak Moses—and used him to free the Israelites and part an entire sea. He used Esther, from the least favored lineage, to change a king's mind and save her people. He used David, the smallest of all his brothers, to kill the giant Goliath and become a king after God's own heart. He used John, a common fisherman, to be His most beloved disciple and be an elder to the early church for decades. He used Paul, a former persecutor and murderer of Christians, to be a major leader for the first followers of Jesus and writer of much of the New Testament letters.

We invite God into the dreams we hold in open hands, as we walk into each of these holidays asking and expecting Him to bring about a better way—one that is so much greater than anything we could ever imagine. We take the first steps, and He leads the path.

BABY STEPS

As I talk to women about making holidays sacred, I see it in their eyes: to change course feels so very overwhelming. Where do you even start? You start in one place and you pick one thing.

I'm an extremist, so I really struggle with this whole baby-step concept. I'm that person who is either 5 percent or 155 percent in. My closest friends and family know to never play a practical joke on me because I don't know how to respond without taking my reciprocal practical joke too far. It's one of the biggest pet peeves about myself, and most hilarious quirks. I have a really hard time with the whole "slow and steady wins the race" mentality.

So when I decided to change course with holidays many years ago, it was a little overwhelming, which kept me from doing anything. Actually, Pinterest kept me from doing anything because they had one million suggestions about everything. It took one search of the word *Advent* on Pinterest for me to quickly resolve to keeping things just as they had always been. And on that Christmas Eve, as I stood there with so many regrets, I knew I missed what was best because I stayed in ignorance, giving in to all-things overwhelming.

Let's not waste another year because these first steps seem too hard.

The very best thing you can do is "baby step" this process. I recommend that you choose one to three things each year and implement that. Get a strong foundation around that tradition and see how it works for you, then the next year implement the following thing. We will walk together through each of the holidays; plus you will create additional references to use for years to come. So all those awesome ideas you hear from others or see on Pinterest, if it inspires without making you crazy, you can jot those down in this book.

Doesn't that sound like a relief? Pressure is off, my friend.

Except there are a few of you who are stubborn and want all the change now. I get it; remember, I'm a fellow extremist. For any woman who has ever gone on a diet (which is most all of us), we know this—you can't lose all the weight on the first day. You can't even lose all the weight in the first month. Those who do lose weight quickly, typically gain most, all, or more back just as quickly because nothing really changed. Those who keep it off are the ones who slowly learned how to change their habits. We are also doing slow, committed change. I know that's not at all what you want to hear, but I wanted to lay all the cards on the table now. We can imagine that by the time we've turned the last page of this book that everything will be better. That we will have magically transformed holidays. I want to say I wish that was true, but I won't. The work is the refining part and it's the beautiful part of the journey too . . . even if it just so happens to be the most annoying part.

When I started working toward losing weight with my nutritionist, Amber, do you know how we started? That's right, one baby step at a time. Week one my goal was to start eating breakfast. I mean, how silly is that? I'm a grown woman—it should be assumed that I can handle eating breakfast. It shouldn't have to be an assignment that includes talking to a nutritionist for an hour and taking an entire week to work on. That is shame, and we already addressed shameful thoughts. So for a week I focused on breakfast. We made a list of three go-to healthy breakfast options. I committed to eat before my kids woke up, since that was one of my issues was not eating until all kids were up, taken care off, off to school, or down for naps. I put myself last and forgot about the basics. Shame kept me from realizing this. Do you know what week two homework was? To start my day with hot tea, instead of three cups of coffee. Ugh, I know. I almost stopped this whole thing. We talked through the benefits of starting your day with hot tea first. So I do that now; I start my day with hot tea, then breakfast, and then I have coffee. She knows that coffee is one of the great loves of my life and that wasn't something I was going to give up, so we kept it. Each week we continued doing one thing and because of that, I'm still doing it all these months later. This hasn't been an extreme change, but a gradual one.

This, my sweet friend, is what I want you to consider doing. It will feel painfully slow at first. However, in five years, ten years, and decades from now when you've reset your entire holiday culture for yourself, your family, and, likely, much of your community, you will be glad you took baby steps instead of sprinted and quit.

Just like my nutritionist let me keep the things I loved, like coffee, I want you to do the same—keep the parts you love, take out the parts that aren't healthy, and add in the things that would make it a "better way." Making holidays more sacred doesn't mean we become one of *those* Christians. You know the type, and we will talk more about them at the end of the book.

FEAR NOT, FOR I HAVE

To close out this chapter, I want you to read Isaiah 43, keeping in mind everything we've discussed: your regrets, His better way, and the baby steps you are about to take. This chapter in the Bible is one of the most life-giving chapters for me and I hope it wildly encourages you. Don't skip this part; take the time to slowly read through it.

As you read, ask your Father to heal the regrets, silence the shame of the enemy, show you a better way, give you the courage and faith to take the next baby steps, and for an increased trust that He will lead you and that He is able. I'm going to encourage you often to write in this book to make it the most awesome holiday resource you've ever had.

- Read through this Scripture once and just hear it.
- Then read it again and circle all the references of God (His name or reference to Him in any context).
- Then read it one last time and underline all the actions He has done, is doing, or will do (for example, in verse 1 you would underline the words "created" and "formed").

But now thus says the LORD, he who created you, O Jacob, he who formed you, O Israel: "Fear not, for I have redeemed you; I have called you by name, you are mine. When you pass through the waters, I will be with you; and through the rivers, they shall not overwhelm you; when you walk through fire you shall not be burned, and the flame shall not consume you. For I am the LORD your God, the Holy One of Israel, your Savior. I give Egypt as your ransom, Cush and Seba in exchange for you. Because you are precious in my eyes, and honored, and I love you, I give men in return for you, peoples in exchange for your life. Fear not, for I am with you; I will bring your offspring from the east, and from the west I will gather you. I will say to the north, Give up, and to the south, Do not withhold; bring my sons from afar and my daughters from the end of the earth, everyone who is called by my name, whom I created for my glory, whom I formed and made."

Bring out the people who are blind, yet have eyes, who are deaf, yet have ears! All the nations gather together, and the peoples assemble. Who among them can declare this, and show us the former things? Let them bring their witnesses to prove them right, and let them hear and say, It is true. "You are my witnesses," declares the LORD, "and my servant whom I have chosen, that you may know and believe me and understand that I am he. Before me no god was formed, nor shall there be any after me. I, I am the LORD, and besides me there is no savior. I declared and saved and proclaimed, when there was no strange god among you; and you are my witnesses," declares the LORD, "and I am God. Also henceforth I am he; there is none who can deliver from my hand; I work, and who can turn it back?" Thus says the LORD, your Redeemer, the Holy One of Israel: "For your sake I send to Babylon and bring them all down as fugitives, even the Chaldeans, in the ships in which they rejoice. I am the LORD, your Holy One, the Creator of Israel, your King." Thus says the LORD, who makes a way in the sea, a path in the mighty waters, who brings forth chariot and horse, army and warrior; they lie down, they cannot rise, they are extinguished, quenched like a wick: "Remember not the former things, nor consider the things of old. Behold, I am doing a new thing; now it springs forth, do you not perceive it? I will make a way in the wilderness and rivers in the desert. The wild beasts will honor me, the jackals and the ostriches, for I give water in the wilderness, rivers in the desert, to give drink to my chosen people, the people whom I formed for myself that they might declare my praise." (Isa. 43:1–21)

We silence those whispers of shame over our regrets with truth—His truth. It's simply not about us or our efforts; it's always been about Him. I hope you were in awe as you circled all those references about Him and underlined all He has or will do.

I want to wrap up this chapter by praying over you, my new friend:

Jesus, would You help my sister to believe this is all true of her. Silence, in the name of Jesus, all those lies of the enemy and accusations she hears from the regrets she has over past holidays. Free her from carrying that any longer. Give her a greater determination to change course than she has ever had before. Help her to desire and believe that there is a better way, more than any thought she could dream or way she could plan. You have said, Father, in Isaiah 55 that Your ways are higher. Help her to take the first step to higher, but keep her eyes fixed on You alone.

Lord, thank You for Your Word and all that Isaiah 43 showed us that You are. We proclaim, Father, that You are the creator of my friend, specifically formed by You. You are her redeemer. You have called her by name. By name, Father, You know and speak about her and to her! You call her "Mine"; she is Yours. You see her walking through the waters, and yet You are with her. You see her when she walks through the fire, and You keep her from being burned or consumed by the flames, even if she is surrounded by them. You say You are the Lord her God, the Holy One. You've exchanged so much for her. You see her as precious and honored and You love her. You don't want her to fear when You tell her You are with her, and You are Father—always with her. You speak in every direction and tell them what to give and want to withhold nothing from her. You've called her by name. You've created her for Your glory. You formed and made her just as she is. You call her Your witness. You say she is Your chosen servant all so that she would know and believe and understand that You indeed are Him, her Father. Would You help her to really know and fully believe and truly understand that You are Him! Lord, remind her that there has never been a God before or after You. Help her not to give her attention or belief to other gods or idols. Help her to know that You are the Lord and there is no one or no thing besides You that will ever save her. You are God. Your hand is faithful and

Your faithfulness is unchanging and reliable. You redeem her—taking what was and making it new. You are the Holy One over my friend, her Creator. You, Father, will make a way in the sea of her life, just as You made a way for Moses. You will cut the path for her—allowing all that she needs to pass. Help her not to dwell on former things, the regrets of the past holidays, or to even think about them. You, Lord, are doing something new! It's already starting! Help her to see it, feel it, and believe it! Remind her that You will make a way in her wilderness, all she doesn't yet see. You make rivers in the desert, taking what seems impossible and bringing not a way out but a way to sustain her as she makes her way through. Lord, You want her to praise You—give her the words to tell You and others how awesome You are!

Jesus, as she continues on through this book, would You lead her? Give her the space and determination to read this book and the discipline and courage to live it out. Surround her by community and family who will do this with her—a new way, a better way. In Jesus' name, I ask all these things. Amen!

LET'S REALLY STAY FRIENDS

Sacredholidays.com // facebook.com/sacredholidays // facebook.com/groups/SacredHolidaysTribe // @sacredholidays

We love you so much, I hope you've heard that throughout this study. We want, more than anything else, to come alongside you during these chaotic and magical holidays and help you know Christ and love others more!

Chat with you soon!

Love you! Mean it.

BECKY KISER + THE SACRED HOLIDAYS TEAM

Made in the USA
Columbia, SC
14 November 2018